for the future

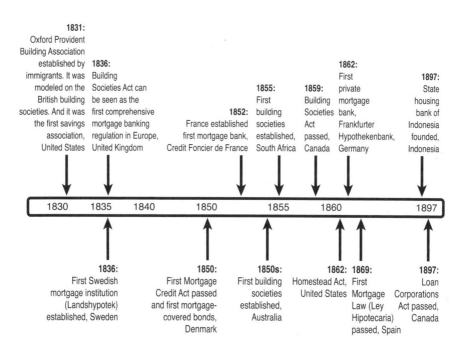

1831:
Oxford Provident Building Association established by immigrants. It was modeled on the British building societies. And it was the first savings association, United States

1836:
Building Societies Act can be seen as the first comprehensive mortgage banking regulation in Europe, United Kingdom

1852:
France established first mortgage bank, Credit Foncier de France

1855:
First building societies established, South Africa

1859:
Building Societies Act passed, Canada

1862:
First private mortgage bank, Frankfurter Hypothekenbank, Germany

1897:
State housing bank of Indonesia founded, Indonesia

| 1830 | 1835 | 1840 | 1850 | 1855 | 1860 | 1897 |

1836:
First Swedish mortgage institution (Landshypotek) established, Sweden

1850:
First Mortgage Credit Act passed and first mortgage-covered bonds, Denmark

1850s:
First building societies established, Australia

1862:
Homestead Act, United States

1869:
First Mortgage Law (Ley Hipotecaria) passed, Spain

1897:
Loan Corporations Act passed, Canada

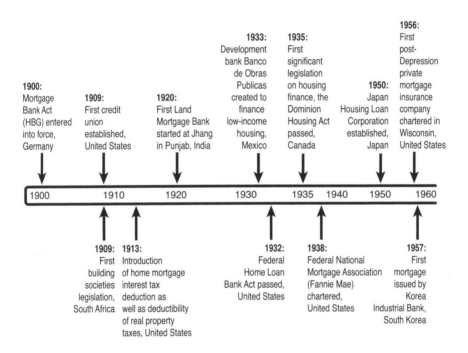

1900:
Mortgage Bank Act (HBG) entered into force, Germany

1909:
First credit union established, United States

1920:
First Land Mortgage Bank started at Jhang in Punjab, India

1933:
Development bank Banco de Obras Publicas created to finance low-income housing, Mexico

1935:
First significant legislation on housing finance, the Dominion Housing Act passed, Canada

1950:
Japan Housing Loan Corporation established, Japan

1956:
First post-Depression private mortgage insurance company chartered in Wisconsin, United States

1900 · 1910 · 1920 · 1930 · 1935 · 1940 · 1950 · 1960

1909:
First building societies legislation, South Africa

1913:
Introduction of home mortgage interest tax deduction as well as deductibility of real property taxes, United States

1932:
Federal Home Loan Bank Act passed, United States

1938:
Federal National Mortgage Association (Fannie Mae) chartered, United States

1957:
First mortgage issued by Korea Industrial Bank, South Korea

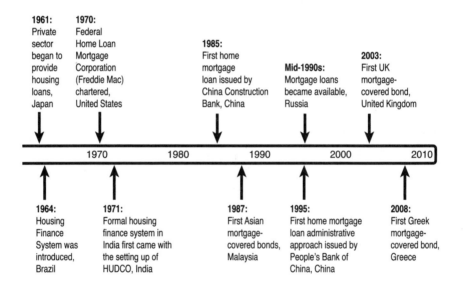

1961: Private sector began to provide housing loans, Japan

1970: Federal Home Loan Mortgage Corporation (Freddie Mac) chartered, United States

1985: First home mortgage loan issued by China Construction Bank, China

Mid-1990s: Mortgage loans became available, Russia

2003: First UK mortgage-covered bond, United Kingdom

1970   1980   1990   2000   2010

1964: Housing Finance System was introduced, Brazil

1971: Formal housing finance system in India first came with the setting up of HUDCO, India

1987: First Asian mortgage-covered bonds, Malaysia

1995: First home mortgage loan administrative approach issued by People's Bank of China, China

2008: First Greek mortgage-covered bond, Greece

Fixing the
Housing Market

Fixing the Housing Market

Financial Innovations for the Future

Franklin Allen
James R. Barth
Glenn Yago

Vice President, Publisher: Tim Moore
Associate Publisher and Director of Marketing: Amy Neidlinger
Executive Editor: Jim Boyd
Editorial Assistant: Pamela Boland
Operations Specialist: Jodi Kemper
Senior Marketing Manager: Julie Phifer
Assistant Marketing Manager: Megan Graue
Cover Designer: Chuti Prasertsith
Managing Editor: Kristy Hart
Senior Project Editor: Lori Lyons
Copy Editor: Krista Hansing Editorial Services
Proofreader: Apostrophe Editing Services
Indexer: Erika Millen
Compositor: Nonie Ratcliff
Manufacturing Buyer: Dan Uhrig

This book is sold with the understanding that neither the authors nor the publisher is engaged in rendering legal, accounting, or other professional services or advice by publishing this book. Each individual situation is unique. Thus, if legal or financial advice or other expert assistance is required in a specific situation, the services of a competent professional should be sought to ensure that the situation has been evaluated carefully and appropriately. The authors and the publisher disclaim any liability, loss, or risk resulting directly or indirectly, from the use or application of any of the contents of this book.

Prentice Hall offers excellent discounts on this book when ordered in quantity for bulk purchases or special sales. For more information, please contact U.S. Corporate and Government Sales, 1-800-382-3419, corpsales@pearsontechgroup.com. For sales outside the U.S., please contact International Sales at international@pearson.com.

Company and product names mentioned herein are the trademarks or registered trademarks of their respective owners.

Pearson Education LTD.
Pearson Education Australia PTY, Limited.
Pearson Education Singapore, Pte. Ltd.
Pearson Education Asia, Ltd.
Pearson Education Canada, Ltd.
Pearson Educatión de Mexico, S.A. de C.V.
Pearson Education—Japan
Pearson Education Malaysia, Pte. Ltd.

Library of Congress Cataloging-in-Publication Data

Allen, Franklin, 1956-

 Fixing the housing market : financial innovations for the future / Franklin Allen, James R. Barth, Glenn Yago.

  p. cm.

 Includes bibliographical references and index.

 ISBN-13: 978-0-13-701160-5 (hardcover : alk. paper)

 ISBN-10: 0-13-701160-1

 1. Housing finance. 2. Global Financial Crisis, 2008-2009. I. Barth, James R. II. Yago, Glenn. III. Title.

 HD7287.55.A45 2012

 332.7'22--dc23

                    2011045176

Contents

Acknowledgments

This volume is the second in our Wharton School Publishing–Milken Institute Series on Financial Innovation. It is dedicated to moving beyond the residential mortgage problems in recent years and looking ahead to new financial innovation solutions for fixing housing markets. From mortgage stones in antiquity to the Homestead Act, building societies, and the emergence of secondary markets in structured-finance products that enable greater access to rental and owner-occupied housing, the requirements for financially and environmentally sustainable buildings to house residential communities is an ongoing challenge. But this is an important objective because it provides an opportunity to create shelter access, jobs, and income and wealth. Demographic factors and changes in cyclical demand have heavily influenced the matching of long-term assets and term maturities of liabilities in residential real estate since human settlement began.

In the first volume, we expressed thanks to the many pioneers of innovation, research, and practice in financial economics. Our gratitude for the thought leadership and practice in financial innovation from these practitioners and researchers applies to this volume as well. We are grateful to many individuals trying to resolve the problems of capital structure, market and regulatory failures, financial product and process engineering, and policy and program development in housing. This includes professionals from government agencies, financial institutions, capital markets, nongovernmental organizations involved in community development finance, and professionals in the housing finance and home building industry. Housing finance depends on a multidisciplinary pool of researchers in urban land use, design, finance, and economics throughout the world; these researchers contributed to our understanding and synthesis of diverse views presented here from the wealth of experience, experiment, failure, and success in building shelter and cities that help build our urban environment as we know it. Housing in the emerging markets represents the hopes and dreams of the residents of an increasingly urbanized world. Realizing those dreams of new homes requires active economic participation and access to housing—a key ingredient in building bridges to a global middle class.

The expertise represented in this volume is too numerous to mention, but we would like to acknowledge those who had a particular influence on our thinking, including Alan Boyce, Shraga Biran, Lewis Ranieri, Michael Milken, Elyse Cherry, Shari Barenbach, Stuart Gabriel, Peter Linneman, Robert Edelstein, Michael Lea, Hernando de Soto, Martin Regalia, Mark Pinsky, Tina Horowitz, Lynn Yin, and Chenying Zhang. Our colleagues at the Milken Institute and the Wharton School at the University of Pennsylvania continue to provide an enthusiastic and committed intellectual environment for research on financial innovations, for which we are grateful. We are very thankful for their interest in and support for this series on applications of financial innovation that grow out of economic and financial theory and research and the ongoing practice of shelter finance represented in this volume. We would also like to acknowledge the support from the Ford Foundation and cooperation of the U.S. Department of Treasury and San Francisco Federal Reserve Bank for their participation in financial innovations labs in housing policy conducted by the Milken Institute. We are particularly grateful to Tong (Cindy) Li, Rick Palacios, Caitlin Maclean, Martha Amram, Apanard (Penny) Prabhavivadhana, Jakob Thomas, Kumiko Green, and Karen Giles for their research and production support, and to James Hankins for his editing of this book. None of the above can be held responsible for mistakes or failings of this work. Our hope is that this book will help facilitate new financial technologies that can be transferred to emerging and troubled developed markets, to improve the affordability of housing and urban revitalization and thus provide for more livable cities and regions throughout the world.

About the Authors

Franklin Allen is the Nippon Life Professor of Finance and Professor of Economics at the Wharton School of the University of Pennsylvania, where he has been on the faculty since 1980. A current codirector of the Wharton Financial Institutions Center, he was formerly vice dean and director of Wharton Doctoral Programs as well as executive editor of the *Review of Financial Studies*, one of the nation's leading academic finance journals. Allen is a past president of the American Finance Association, the Western Finance Association, the Society for Financial Studies, and the Financial Intermediation Research Society. His main areas of interest are corporate finance, asset pricing, financial innovation, comparative financial systems, and financial crises. He is a coauthor, with Richard Brealey and Stewart Myers, of the eighth through tenth editions of the textbook *Principles of Corporate Finance*. In addition, he is coauthor, with Glenn Yago, of *Financing the Future: Market-Based Innovations for Growth*. Allen received his doctorate from Oxford University.

James R. Barth is the Lowder Eminent Scholar in Finance at Auburn University and a Senior Finance Fellow at the Milken Institute. His research focuses on financial institutions and capital markets, both domestic and global, with special emphasis on regulatory issues. He has served as leader of an international team advising the People's Bank of China on banking reform and traveled to China, India, Russia, and Egypt to lecture on various financial topics for the U.S. State Department. He was interviewed about the financial crisis of 2007 to 2009 by the Financial Crisis Inquiry Commission and the Congressional Oversight Panel. An appointee of Presidents Ronald Reagan and George H. W. Bush, Barth was chief economist of the Office of Thrift Supervision and previously the Federal Home Loan Bank Board. He has also held the positions of professor of economics at George Washington University, associate director of the economics program at the National Science Foundation, and Shaw Foundation Professor of Banking and Finance at Nanyang Technological University. He has been a visiting scholar at the U.S. Congressional Budget

Office, Federal Reserve Bank of Atlanta, Office of the Comptroller of the Currency, and the World Bank. Barth has testified before the U.S. House and Senate banking committees on several occasions. He has authored more than 200 articles in professional journals and has written and edited several books, including *The Rise and Fall of the U.S. Mortgage and Credit Markets: A Comprehensive Analysis of the Meltdown; Rethinking Bank Regulation: Till Angels Govern; Financial Restructuring and Reform in Post-WTO China; China's Emerging Markets: Challenges and Opportunities; The Great Savings and Loan Debacle;* and *The Reform of Federal Deposit Insurance.* His most recent book is *Guardians of Finance: Making Regulators Work for Us.* Barth is the coeditor of *The Journal of Financial Economic Policy* and overseas associate editor of *The Chinese Banker.* He has been quoted in news publications ranging from *The New York Times, The Financial Times,* and *The Wall Street Journal* to *Time* and *Newsweek.* In addition, he has appeared on such broadcast programs as *Newshour, Good Morning America, Moneyline,* Bloomberg News, Fox Business News, and National Public Radio. Barth is also included in *Who's Who in Economics: A Biographical Dictionary of Major Economists, 1700 to 1995.*

Glenn Yago is Senior Fellow/Senior Director at the Milken Institute and its Israel Center. He is also a visiting professor at Hebrew University of Jerusalem where he directs the Koret–Milken Institute Fellows program. Yago is Founder of the Institute's Financial Innovations Labs®, which focus on the innovative use of finance to solve long-standing economic development, social, and environmental challenges. His financial research and demonstration projects have contributed to policy innovations fostering the democratization of capital to traditionally underserved markets and entrepreneurs in the United States and around the world. Yago is the coauthor of several books, including *The Rise and Fall of the U. S. Mortgage and Credit Markets; Global Edge; Restructuring Regulation and Financial Institutions;* and *Beyond Junk Bonds.* In addition, he is coauthor, with Franklin Allen, of *Financing the Future: Market-Based Innovations for Growth.* He was formerly a professor at the State University of New York at Stony Brook and at the City University of New York Graduate Center's Ph.D. Program in Economics. Yago earned his Ph.D. at the University of Wisconsin, Madison.

About the Milken Institute

A nonprofit, nonpartisan think tank, the Milken Institute believes in the power of capital markets to solve urgent social and economic challenges. Its mission is to improve lives around the world by advancing innovative economic and policy solutions that create jobs, widen access to capital, and enhance health.

We produce rigorous, independent economic research—and maximize its impact by convening global leaders from the worlds of business, finance, policy, academia, and philanthropy. These collaborations between the public and private sectors are meant to transform ideas into action. Together we advance strategies to solve today's most urgent policy challenges.

1

Housing Crises Go Global:
The Boom, the Bust, and Beyond

Global Housing Crisis and
the Demand for Shelter Capital

Rapid population growth and urbanization accompanied by a global housing crisis are creating massive shelter poverty in an era of financial chaos and emerging social and political instability. The shelter crises are more visible than ever as rural areas empty and megacities abound with unregulated housing districts circling urban cores.

In many developing world capitals, more than half of the housing stock is informal or squatter settlements without clear property rights or access to capital for housing or home improvements. Slums are the fastest-growing housing stock in the world (25% annually). According to United Nations statistics, more than 1.6 billion people live in substandard housing (32% of the global urban population), and that will exceed 2 billion over the next ten years without major new solutions.[1]

In the face of this, the United Nations Millennium Development goals call for a significant improvement in the lives of at least 100 million slum dwellers by 2020. If that goal is considered a victory for international housing policy efforts, you would have to wonder what a surrender would look like. This book explores how public and private investment trends and financial innovations can find scalable solutions to these global shelter needs.

In this context, the litany of data documenting housing dislocation grows daily. Housing markets are teetering in the U.S. and around the world. Financial crises have compounded the shelter problems in Greece, Spain, Italy, Ireland, Portugal, and other countries.[2] Homebuilder sentiment remains at a historical low point as borrowers face difficulty getting mortgages from wary banks. The number of lenders seizing properties broke records in 2011. The bloated supply of unsold homes lingers, with ownerless houses at their highest since records have been kept. Foreclosure rates continue to soar.

Among 39 countries surveyed on house prices, 26 recorded price drops and 18 experienced accelerating rates of decline that are closely related to burgeoning debt and financial crises worldwide.[3] The shadow of falling home prices is accompanied by a decrease in consumption spending, low consumer and producer confidence, an ongoing credit crunch, and worsening unemployment.

In this book, we look beyond the booms, bubbles, and inevitable busts of real estate markets to examine prospective solutions to finance housing's future. Always, though, before moving forward, we have to understand the past.

Overview of Early Shelter and Its Financing

Before the rise of modern civilizations and coincident with the agricultural revolution during the Neolithic period, human settlements began to take on more permanent structural forms as the means and methods of constructing dwellings emerged throughout the world.[4] The earliest homes, from pre-Roman British dwellings, to African roundhouses, to Mesopotamian reconstructions, have some remarkable spatial and construction similarities that resemble a modest three-bedroom home for a family today. Simple technology combined with minimal mobilization of resources enabled a sedentary culture to develop.

Design innovations contributed to the evolution of housing as human inventiveness and vision worked to overcome the scarcity of shelter. From the earliest permanent dwellings; to urban homes in Mesopotamia, Egypt, the Indus Civilization, and China; to the convergence of industrialization and urbanization in the modern city, the diversity of housing designs has led to increasingly complex patterns of human settlement that can now be explored from Google Earth. In the twenty-first century, as the world has finally achieved majority urbanization, the need for financial innovations for housing continues unabated.

Perhaps not surprisingly, innovations in housing construction have not always been successful. This has been the case even when some of the world's greatest inventors tried their hand at reinventing housing. More than a hundred years ago, for example, Thomas Edison patented a cast-iron system for mass-producing concrete homes, but it never gained critical mass. Even though Buckminster Fuller's steel hexagonal homes in the 1920s were nearly half the cost of a conventional bungalow, they attracted no customers. Walter Gropius, father of the Bauhaus movement, was part of a failed effort in the 1940s to package and deliver prefabricated homes.[5]

As the demographically driven demand for housing and housing finance increased over the years, the lack of major production and financial innovations challenged the ability to meet growing needs.

Economics of Housing

Similarly, efforts to increase homeownership or bolster the supply of rental housing have met with both success and failure. Inventive modes of housing finance do not always succeed. Clearly, the learning curve in developing well-functioning real estate markets has been quite steep. Again, real estate as an asset class is associated with financial crises.

The character of housing is multidimensional, an important factor to consider when seeking financial solutions. A home can be viewed as a shelter, an investment, or simply a product—the ultimate consumer durable.

From their earliest beginnings, homes have been the largest investment most individuals and their families make. Until the recent price collapse in the United States and other countries, they were also the most passive of investments.

Economic theory suggests several factors driving housing demand:

- Physical characteristics of housing (rooms, facilities, water and sewage, location, construction, and so on)
- Prices for residential services (such as the value-to-rent ratio of owning versus renting)
- Investment components (capital gains in real income)
- Current and permanent income characteristics[6]

Even after the recent housing crisis, real estate is one of the largest businesses in the world. Buying, selling, and renting properties and the related benefits to owner-occupiers accounts for 15% of the gross domestic product (GDP) of developed countries and two-thirds of the tangible stock of most economies.[7]

The importance of housing wealth cannot be understated. In Europe and Australia, housing accounts for 40% to 60% of total household wealth, while in America, it is about 30%.[8] Changes in such wealth can have significant effects on consumer spending and, therefore, overall economic activity. In particular, financial and real losses can be magnified when property prices fall from historic highs.[9]

Of the components of GDP, residential investment is always an early warning sign of recessions. As Robert Shiller has noted, "Residential construction as a percentage of gross domestic product has had a prominent peak before almost every recession since 1950."[10]

The First Housing Finance Innovations

The credit mechanisms that have amplified the growth and economic effects of the housing sector have a long and, at times, unpleasant history.

The first evidence of mortgages was *horoi,* or "mortgage stones," in ancient Athens (see Figure 1.1). These were markers used to indicate that a property was mortgaged and to identify the creditors.[11] By the late twelfth century, mortgages had reappeared in England in the form of common-law instruments to enable the purchase and sale of property. In a property sale, lenders could recover real estate debts that were not paid.

Figure 1.1 Mortgage boundary stone, Athens agora market, 215 B.C.

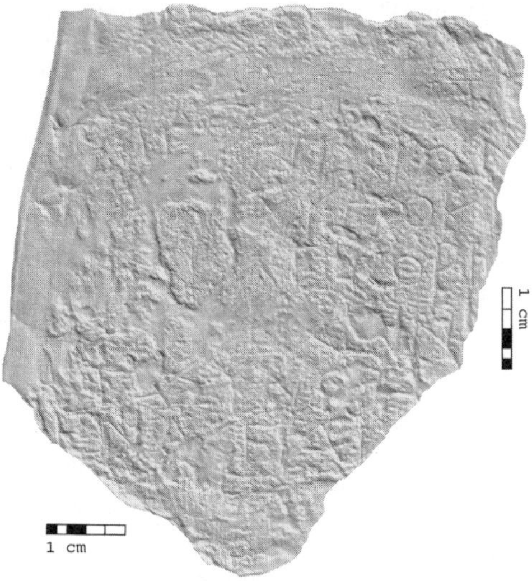

Source: Center for Epigraphical and Paleographical Studies, Ohio State University.

Initially, ownership rights of property were extended from the earth's center to the sky. Later, however, they were constrained to surface rights, as "air rights" for further vertical development and their transfer increased in value through increasingly dense urban settlement.

Reverse mortgages, which provided benefits for elderly owners by allowing them to extract equity, did not appear until the 1930s. The ability to borrow against the equity in homes came later. Table 1.1 provides selected developments in the housing and mortgage markets in various countries over the past millennia.

Table 1.1 Historical Developments in Housing and Mortgage Markets

Year	Country	Comment
2650–2575 B.C.	Egypt	Property mortgage used in the Old Kingdom.
1000 B.C.	China	Pawnshop mortgages used.
400 B.C.	Greece	Mortgages and personal loans secured by real estate.
1644	China	Emergence of mortgage loan industry during Qing Dynasty.

Year	Country	Comment
1700	Denmark	First mortgage institution funded as an association.
1769	Prussia	Start of the mortgage covered bond (Pfandbriefe) market.
1775	United Kingdom	First known building society for housing finance formed.
1797	Denmark	First Danish mortgage bank.
1831	United States	Oxford Provident Building Association established by immigrants. It was modeled on the British building societies and was the first savings association.
1836	Sweden	First Swedish mortgage institution, Landshypotek, established.
1836	United Kingdom	Building Societies Act becomes first comprehensive mortgage banking regulation in Europe.
1850	Denmark	First Mortgage Credit Act passed.
1852	France	France established first mortgage bank, Credit Foncier de France.
1850s	Australia	First building societies established.
1855	South Africa	First building societies established.
1859	Canada	Building Societies Act passed.
1861	Spain	First Mortgage Law (Ley Hipotecaria) passed.
1862	Germany	First private mortgage bank, Frankfurter Hypothekenbank.
1897	Canada	Loan Corporations Act passed.
1897	Indonesia	State housing bank of Indonesia founded.
1900	Germany	Mortgage Bank Act (HBG) entered into force.
1909	South Africa	First building societies legislation created.
1909	United States	First credit union established.
1920	India	First Land Mortgage Bank started at Jhang in Punjab.
1932	United States	Federal Home Loan Bank Act passed.
1933	Mexico	Development bank Banco de Obras Publicas created to finance low-income housing.
1935	Canada	First significant legislation on housing finance, the Dominion Housing Act, passed.

Year	Country	Comment
1938	United States	Federal National Mortgage Association (Fannie Mae) chartered.
1950	Japan	Japan Housing Loan Corporation established.
1957	South Korea	First mortgage issued by Korea Industrial Bank.
1961	Japan	Private-sector began to provide housing loans.
1964	Brazil	Housing Finance System was introduced.
1970	United States	Federal Home Loan Mortgage Corporation (Freddie Mac) chartered.
1971	India	Formal housing finance system in India first came with the setting up of HUDCO.
1985	China	First home mortgage loan issued by China Construction Bank.
1995	China	First home mortgage loan administrative approach issued by People's Bank of China.
Mid-1990s	Russia	Mortgage loans became available in Russia.

Sources: *Mistress of the House, Mistress of Heaven: Women in Ancient Egypt,* Anne K. Capel, Glenn Markoe, Cincinnati Art Museum, Brooklyn Museum, 1996. http://om-paramapoonya. hubpages.com/hub/Pawnshop-Loans. *A History of Interest Rates,* 4th ed., Sidney Homer and Richard Sylla, 2005. *Securitization of the Financial Instrument of the Future,* Vinod Kothari, 2006. *Improving Unification of Euro Debt Markets: A Concrete Case Study of Covered Bonds,* AMTE Final Report. 2005. *Housing Finance Policy in Emerging Markets,* Loïüc Chiquier, Michael J. Lea, 2009. *Mortgage Finance in Denmark,* Torben Gjede, 1997. *National Housing Finance Systems: A Comparative Study,* Mark Boléat, 1985. *Scandi Covered Bond Handbook 2010,* Christian Riemann-Andersen and Kristian Myrup Pedersen, 2010. *The History of Building Societies in the UK,* The Building Societies Association, 2001. *European Covered Bond Fact Book,* 2006. Credit Union and Building Society Group, www.comesbacktoyou.com.au/what-are-credit-unions-building-societies-/history-of-credit-unions-building-societies. *Real Property Law—Spain Report,* Pedro Garrido, 2009. *The German Pfandbrief: A benchmark for Europe,* Verband Deutscher Hypothekenbanken and Association of German Mortgage Banks, 1998. *Handbook on the History of European Banks,* Manfred Pohl, Sabine Freitag, and European Association for Banking History, 1994. http://blog.sina.com.cn/s/blog_4865b35c0100gy57.html. *Housing Finance and Mortgage-Backed Securities in Mexico,* L. Zanforlin and Marco Espinosa-Vega, 2008. *Housing Finance in Japan,* Miki Seko, 1994. *Wu Xiaoling: Strengthening China's Financial Industry in the Process of Opening up 2006,* China Housing Finance Report, People's Bank of China, 2004 (www.pbc.gov. cn/history_file/files/att_15025_1.pdf).

Innovations in housing and expansion of ownership track closely with land reform. In the eighteenth century, when this process began to emerge, most land was "entailed." This meant that the landed gentry and noblemen owned all real estate in perpetuity.

Early land developers crafted financial contracts that were rolling options—the real estate investor bought not an entire large tract, but a segment for development and resale accompanied by a purchased option for the adjacent segment. The pioneer in this effort was John Wood and his son, whose projects in Bath, England, used this method to integrate individual housing units and related commercial space to develop the city. Wood went beyond the city limits of Bath to an area unencumbered by regulations and leased land for 99 years, with each lease based on the performance of the development of the previous one. By utilizing options, he was able to circumvent land laws, raise debt and equity financing, and lease and manage related properties in Bath developments. This was the beginning of urban real estate development and residential housing finance as we know it today.[12]

Industrial Revolution and Housing Finance

Simultaneously, with the origins of real estate development in the late eighteenth century came the rise of building societies accompanying the metalworking industry around Birmingham, England. In the coffee shops and taverns where ideas were freely exchanged, specialized savings organizations were founded to promote homebuilding.[13] While most early building societies were initially self-terminating, with the final house built by a remaining member, permanent building societies emerged to become more sustainable financial institutions.

The founding of today's U.S. savings and loans in the early 1830s began with the legacy of early British settlers. They used their familiarity with British building societies to establish similar lending operations in the United States. The development of savings institutions grew through these building and loan societies and later through mutual savings banks in 1816 with the founding of the Provident Institution Savings of Boston, as is more fully discussed in Chapter 2, "Building Blocks of Modern Housing Finance."

Mutual savings banks were owned by their depositors rather than by stockholders. Therefore, any profits belonged to the depositors. In their early years, most of the funds deposited in mutual savings banks had to be invested in municipal bonds that financed the growth of cities—hence, the link between infrastructure and residential expansion was ensured. At the end of the Civil War, about one million people had deposited approximately $250 million in 317 U.S. savings banks. By 1900, more than six million depositors had deposited nearly $2.5 billion in 1,000 banks.[14]

The building and loan associations, in contrast, were created to promote homeownership. The number of associations and assets grew dramatically through the end of the 1800s. Eventually, the building societies took on some aspects of savings banks. They extended loans to building association members who did not have significant funds on deposit to borrow for a home.

Although mutual savings banks and building and loan societies retained individual characteristics, they were often lumped together. When Congress passed the Wilson Tariff Act in 1894 to tax the net income of corporations, building and loan associations and other businesses that made loans only to their shareholders were excluded from taxation. That began a series of provisions granting special legal consideration to savings and loans and the provision of financing for homeownership.

Not surprisingly, other financial innovations arose with the massive shift in structural demand for capital in housing, driven by rapid industrialization and urbanization that accompanied the economic changes of the late eighteenth century. In 1769, Frederick the Great of Prussia structured the first covered bonds in the aftermath of the Seven Years War to ease the credit shortage in agriculture, but he later extended the concept to residential and commercial real estate. Issued by banks and secured by a pool of mortgages, covered bonds resemble mortgage-backed securities, with the exception that bondholders have recourse to the underlying collateral of those bonds because the mortgages stay on the issuing bank's balance sheet.[15]

Table 1.2 shows the spread of the use of covered bonds to finance homeownership in different countries over time. The practice has been largely restricted to European countries; the spread to Canada and United States is a recent development. These bonds are the primary source of mortgage funding for European banks, but compared to the securitization used by banks in the U.S., covered bonds have a cost disadvantage due to greater capital requirements.[16]

Table 1.2   Mortgage Covered Bond Use in Countries Over Time

First ... mortgage covered bond	Country	Year	Year	Country	Start / First ...
First Danish mortgage covered bond	Denmark	1850	1769	Prussia	Start of the mortgage covered bond (Pfandbriefe) market
First Asian mortgage covered bond	Malaysia	1987	1930	Switzerland	First Swiss mortgage covered bond
First Hungarian mortgage covered bond	Hungary	1998	1996	Czech Republic	First Czech mortgage covered bond
First Baltic mortgage covered bond	Latvia	1999	1999	France	First French mortgage covered bond (obligations foncières)
First Spanish mortgage covered bond (Cédulas Hipotecarias)	Spain	1999	1999	Slovakia	First Slovak mortgage covered bond
First Bulgarian mortgage covered bond	Bulgaria	2001	2000	Poland	First Polish mortgage covered bond
			2003	United Kingdom	First UK mortgage covered bond
First Irish mortgage covered bond	Ireland	2004	2004	Finland	First Finnish mortgage covered bond
			2004	Lithuania	First Lithuanian mortgage covered bond
			2005	Netherlands	First Dutch mortgage covered bond

First mortgage covered bond event	Country	Year	Year	Country	First mortgage covered bond event
First Portuguese mortgage covered bond (Obrigações Hipotecárias)	Portugal			Luxembourg	First Luxembourgian mortgage-backed securitization (Lettres de Gage hypothecaires)
First U.S. mortgage covered bond	United States	2006	2006	Sweden	First Swedish mortgage covered bond
First Norwegian mortgage covered bond	Norway	2007	2007	Canada	First Canadian mortgage covered bond
				Russia	First Russian mortgage covered bond
First Italian mortgage covered bond	Italy	2008	2008	Greece	First Greek mortgage covered bond
			2009	Korea	First Korean mortgage covered bond
First New Zealand mortgage covered bond	New Zealand	2010			

Source: Milken Institute, *Capital Access Index*, 2005. Information for Denmark is from the European Covered Bond Council, *European Covered Bond Fact Book*, 2010.

Figure 1.2 (a-c) shows the extent to which the mortgage-backed covered bonds played a role in financing homeownership in 2009. Denmark is noteworthy, with covered bonds accounting for 100% of residential loans outstanding and representing more than 140% of the country's GDP. In the United States, covered bonds are a new development and, thus, still relatively unimportant in financing homeownership.

Figure 1.2   The role of covered bonds in selected countries, 2009.

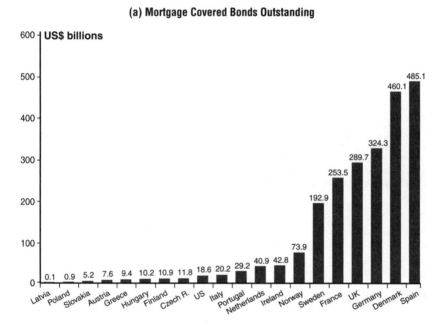

(a) Mortgage Covered Bonds Outstanding

(b) Mortgage-Backed Covered Bonds as Percentage of Residential Loans Outstanding

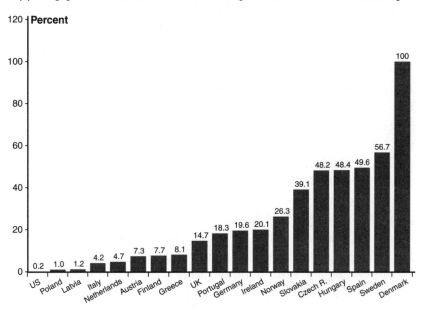

(c) Mortgage-Backed Covered Bonds as Percentage of Nominal GDP

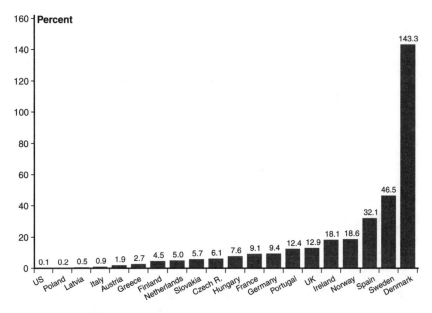

Source: Hypostat, 2009.

Even as urbanization and residential development grew in the eighteenth and nineteenth centuries throughout Europe and the United States, agriculture drove economic growth. Homeownership accompanied reform and expansion of landownership for farming. By 1890 in the United States, two-thirds of all farm housing was owner-occupied; this figure increased throughout the twentieth century. At the same time, homeownership was less prevalent in urban areas. As it became more prevalent, the overall homeownership rate increased from 45% at the beginning of the twentieth century to a range of 60% to 70% by 1960 and has remained at that level ever since (see Figure 1.3).[17] Costs associated with homeownership represent a large and growing portion of consumer spending, especially since the turn of the twentieth century, as the homeownership rate increased, the size of homes expanded, and home prices trended upward. Possession of land and property, especially homes, reinforced some main drivers of nation building: thrift, industriousness, geographical and occupational mobility, citizenship, and economic security.

Figure 1.3 U.S. homeownership rate, 1900 to Q1 2011.

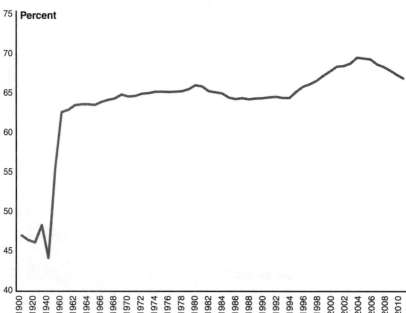

Note: Data from 1910–1960 is for decades, with annual data thereafter.

Source: U.S. Census Bureau.

From Thomas Jefferson, to Andrew Jackson, to Abraham Lincoln, the democratic assumption was that if most citizens had the opportunity to become farmers or independent artisans and proprietors, they would acquire the values, habits, and discipline required to create a viable democracy. Politicians and economists in this tradition believed that the best way to combine a democratic government with a market society was to make sure that productive assets were distributed widely. This goal became increasingly difficult to achieve after the Civil War.

Let's next consider the American economy during the late colonial and early national periods. By the end of the eighteenth century, soil exhaustion caused by tobacco planting and European demands for grains created an extraordinary opportunity for ordinary men to produce for trade. The expansion of international commerce created the material base for a social vision of a democratic nation that had little to do with elitist notions of antiquity, the Renaissance, or the mercantilism of Europe.

The surge in demand brought about by trade increased commercial activities in cities and fueled population growth and westward expansion for 30 years after the American Revolution. Jefferson's vision was democratic, capitalistic, and commercial, linking his interpretation of economic development and how it related to his political goals.[18] Access to farmland was not to shelter a traditional way of life but to apply scientific advances in cultivation, processing, marketing, and finance to enhance agricultural profitability.

Appleby explains it this way:

> *It was exactly the promise of progressive agricultural development that fueled his hopes that ordinary men might escape the tyranny of their social superiors both as employers and magistrates. More than most democratic reformers, he recognized that hierarchy rested on economic relations and deference to the past as well as formal privilege and social custom.*[19]

Access to capital in the form of land for the individual owners, opening markets globally for their product, committing funds to internal improvements, and opposing fiscal measures that hurt taxpayers were all part of Jefferson's policies. Limiting formal authority, deferring to individual freedom, and making a commitment to growth through access to economic opportunity were the keys to economic and political democracy. These notions were the very definition of *Americanism,* a term that Jefferson coined and counterposed to *aristocracy.* He argued consistently against the dominance of a new elite of wealth and privilege and gave high priority to laws that would prevent the concentration of landed wealth. In this context, land reform and home finance merged in public and financial policies and programs.

One concern was that the Jeffersonian and Jacksonian ideals of independent economic citizens could not be realized, given the requirements of industrial production. Most Americans rejected industrial wage labor as a permanent status. As Christopher Lasch recounts in his history of political thought during nineteenth-century America:

> *Even when Americans finally came to accept the wage systems as an indispensable feature of capitalism, they continued to comfort themselves with the thought that no one had to occupy the condition of a wage earner indefinitely—that each successive wave of immigrants, starting at the bottom, would eventually climb the ladder of success into the proprietary class…permanent status as wage workers…simply could not be reconciled with the American Dream as it was conventionally understood.*[20]

Focusing on land and homeownership, the Homestead Movement was consistent with the Jeffersonian response to this situation. It was geared to opening opportunities for would-be farmers in an age when this occupation was still considered the norm. Ever since the passage of the Land Ordinance of 1785 and the Land Act of 1796, the government provided assistance to settlers in the form of low-priced land. Other acts followed with regularity, such as the Preemption Act of 1841, which permitted would-be settlers to stake claims on most surveyed lands and to buy up to 160 acres for a minimum price of $1.25 per acre.

In 1862, Lincoln signed into law the Homestead Act. Under its terms, any citizen or person intending to become a citizen who headed a family and was over the age of 21 could receive 160 acres of land, with clear title to be conveyed after five years and payment of a registration fee.[21] As an alternative, after six months, the land could be bought for $1.60 an acre. Housing and landownership became common American goals.[22]

On January 1, 1863, Daniel Freeman and 417 others filed homestead claims, and more pioneers followed. By 1934, more than 1.6 million homestead applications had been filed, and more than 270 million acres (representing 10% of the U.S. land mass) passed to individuals in the largest capital distribution measure in public policy.[23] The ethos and purpose of this infused housing policy for years to come.

Considerable restrictions limited the ability of agricultural and industrial workers to access capital and asset markets throughout the nineteenth century. Aside from saving accounts and insurance policies, real estate in the form of houses and lots was a new investment objective of savers.

Without large-scale pension plans, homes were a major repository of wealth, and owner-occupied homes could also become a source of income through rentals and boarding. The choice of home tenure—between renting and owning—emerged in this social, political, and economic context as property markets grew in the nineteenth century with industrialization. Wealth accumulation became concentrated in real property as society became more urban and less rural, and with the associated increasing homeownership rate. These developments set the stage for the genesis of modern housing finance.

In the coming chapters, we outline the market structure, regulatory environment, and banking and financial challenges that formed the environment for the building blocks of housing finance. We examine what went wrong in the recent housing crisis and the variation between countries in developed and emerging markets. Finally, we examine future innovations to bridge market gaps in financing that led to the global housing crisis and the lessons learned for more robust, stable, and sustainable housing markets.

Endnotes

1 UN-Habitat, *State of the World's Cities 2010–2011, Cities for All: Bridging the Urban Divide,* United Nations, 2011.

2 Ashok Bardhan, Robert Edelstein, and Cynthia Kroll (eds.), *Global Housing Markets: Crises, Policies, and Institutions* (New York: Wiley, 2011).

3 Global Property Guide, Investment Analysis, August 26, 2011. www.globalpropertyguide.com/investment-analysis/Global-housing-markets-under-pressure-says-Global-Property-Guide.

4 Gerhard Bersu, "Excavations at Little Woodbury, Wilshire. Part 1, the Settlement Revealed by Excavation," *Proceedings of the Prehistoric Society* 6 (1940): 30–111; Norbert Schoenauer, *6,000 Years of Housing* (New York: W.W. Norton, 2000): 100–122.

5 Witold Rybczynski, "Design and Innovation and the Single-Family House," *Zell/Lurie Real Estate Review and Makeshift Metropolis* (New York: Scribner, 2010).

6 Allen C. Goodman, "An Econometric Model of Housing Price, Permanent Income, Tenure Choice and Housing Demand," *Journal of Urban Economics*, 23, no. 1 (1986): 155–67.

7 Pam Woodall, "House of Cards," *Economist* (May 31, 2003): Vol. 367, Issue 8326, p. 3.

8 Eric Belsky and Joel Prakken, *Housing Wealth Effects: Housing's Impact on Wealth Accumulation, Wealth Distribution and Consumer Spending,* Joint Center for Housing, Harvard University (December 2004).

9 Robert J. Shiller, *Understanding Recent Trends in House Prices and Home Ownership,* Economics Department Working Paper no. 28, Yale University (October 2007).

10 *Ibid.*

11 John V.A. Fine, *Horoi: Studies in Mortgage, Real Security, and Land Tenure in Ancient Athens, Hesperia,* Supplement IX, American School of Classical Studies in Athens, 1951.

12 Harvey Rabinowitz, "The Woods at Bath: Pioneers of Real Estate Development," Zell/Lurie Real Estate Center, *Wharton Real Estate Review* (Fall 2002): 65–71.

13 Herbert Ashworth, The Building Society Story (London: Franey and Co., 1980).

14 James Barth, Susanne Trimbath, and Glenn Yago, *The Savings and Loan Crisis* (New York: Kluwer, 2004) xxvii–xxix.

15 Franklin Allen and Glenn Yago, *Financing the Future* (New York: Pearson, 2010): 106; Henry Paulson, *Best Practices for Residential Covered Bonds,* U.S. Treasury Department (July 2008): 7–11.

16 For further discussion, see Ben S. Bernanke, "The Future of Mortgage Finance in the United States," *The B.E. Journal of Economic Analysis & Policy,* 9, no. 3 (2009):Article 2.

17 According to Williams J. Collins and Robert A. Margo ("Race and Home Ownership," NBER Working Paper no. 7277, August 1999, p. 14), "[I]n 1900, only 16 percent of all white male household heads held a mortgage and only 6 percent of blacks did, but by 1990, 57 percent of whites held a mortgage compared to 43 percent of blacks." It might also be noted that the rate of owner occupancy for African-Americans in 1870 was 8 percent, whereas it had increased to 54 percent in 2007. (See Williams J. Collins and Robert A. Margo, "Race and Home Ownership from the Civil War to the Present," NBER Working Paper no. 16,665, January 2011.

18 J.G.A. Pocock, *Machiavellian Moment: Florentine Political Thought and the Atlantic Republican Tradition* (Princeton, N.J.: Princeton University Press, 1975): 268.

19 Joyce Appleby, *Liberalism and Republicanism in the Historical Imagination* (Cambridge: Harvard University Press, 1992): 269.

20 Christopher Lasch, *The True and Only Heaven* (New York: Basic Books, 1992): 276. See also Lawrence Goodwyn, *Democratic Promise* (New York: Oxford University Press, 1976).

21 Title insurance firms identify mortgage investors and property owners' losses created by defective property titles. Title insurance was created in the United States as early as 1883. (See Dwight Jaffee, "Monoline Restrictions, with Applications to Mortgage Insurance and Title Insurance," *Review of Industrial Organization* 28, 2006: 83–108.)

22 D.M. Frederiksen ("Mortgage Banking in America," *Journal of Political Economy* 2 (2), 1984: 203–234) points out, "Probably the origin of most of these companies [mortgage banking companies] is closely connected with the homestead laws, most of their business having been the making of loans to the new settlers as soon as these had lived long enough on their land to obtain a patent from the Government."

23 U.S. National Archives and Records Administration, "The Homestead Act of 1862," June 30, 2010.

2

Building Blocks of Modern Housing Finance[1]

For many people, homeownership is the "American Dream," as well as an indicator of status, position, and individual identity. But for most people, the dream can't come true without taking advantage of lending practices that have evolved in the U.S. since pre-Civil War days, with the birth of the savings and loan industry.

But first, how does America stack up against other nations in terms of home ownership? The answer to that question has varied over time.

In 1890, the U.S. homeownership rate was at 17.9%, compared to 6.7% for Europeans. By the middle of the twentieth century, that rate had risen above 61% in the U.S., but European countries were gaining as well. Their rates were 50% for Belgium, 33% for France, 13% for Germany, 26% for Sweden, and 43% for the United Kingdom.[2]

Figure 2.1 shows more recent data, with homeownership rates varying from a low of 38% in Switzerland to a high of 97% in Lithuania. Of the 46 countries in the figure, only Switzerland and Germany (43%) fell below 50%. This has been attributed to cultural factors, very low rents, and conservative mortgage lending.[3] Italy, Greece, and Spain have much higher rates of homeownership, reflecting cultural values, discriminatory policies toward private rental housing, and weaker support of "social" rental housing (low-cost public housing owned and managed by government or nonprofit organizations).[4] Fisher and Jaffe have found that, even though several partial factors are associated with high or low rates of homeownership, no single explanation can account for all global patterns. In their words, "any explanation of worldwide homeownership rates must be limited from a generalizable proposition to an anecdotal explanation with limited empirical content."[5]

Figure 2.1 Homeownership rates (%) around the world.

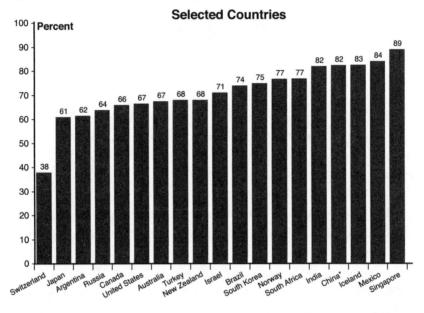

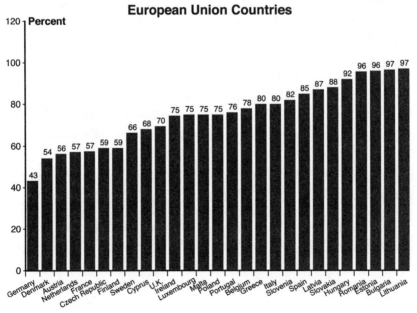

* Homeownership rate only for households that have hukou. (Hukou are people with official registration at cities of residence.)

Note: Based on the latest available data from sources listed below. In countries such as Brazil, where there are favelas, it is not clear exactly how these are treated in terms of the homeownership rate that is provided. Also, it is not clear in another country such as South Africa what is included or excluded in the homeownership rate. The sources listed do not always provide sufficient detail to elaborate on these issues.

Sources: EMF Hypostat (2009) for E.U. countries and Iceland, Russia, Norway, and Turkey; Whitehead (2010) for Australia and Canada; Pollock (2010) for Japan, Israel, New Zealand, and Singapore; U.S. Census Bureau for United States; Euroconstruct (2008) for Switzerland; Gao (2010) for China; United Nations (2001) for Argentina, Brazil, South Korea, and South Africa; and Soula Proxenos (2002) for India.

Figure 2.2 provides information on the ratio of home mortgage debt to gross domestic product (GDP), to accompany the homeownership rates just discussed. As you can see, Switzerland has the highest ratio, even though it has the lowest homeownership rate among the countries in the figure. This reflects a high cost of housing due to substantial increases in housing prices over the past decade and a sizable group of wealthy domestic and foreign-born (often transient) individuals who can afford more expensive homes. Germany has a mortgage debt–to–GDP ratio that is relatively low, reflecting its low rate of homeownership. Overall, the ratio for the 27 European Union countries was 52% in 2009, compared to a U.S. ratio of 67%.

According to Bardhan and Edelstein, "The large differences in the national mortgage markets reflect the fact that mortgage markets retain strong national characteristics…as a result of the differences in the historical, demographic, political and regulatory environments in which mortgage lenders operate."[6]

In some countries, such as France, mortgage interest is not subsidized, yet the rental market is subsidized and heavily regulated. This policy contributes to lower homeownership rates, which, in turn, leads to lower mortgage debt–to–GDP ratios.[7]

More generally, as urban property values increase and more developed mortgage capital markets emerge in cities, a higher proportion of homes can be financed by mortgages in areas of rapid urbanization and industrialization. In this way, homes not only become secure shelter, but also provide potential income (through rentals and boarding) and serve as collateral for borrowing.

Figure 2.2   Home mortgage debt to GDP (%) in countries around the world.

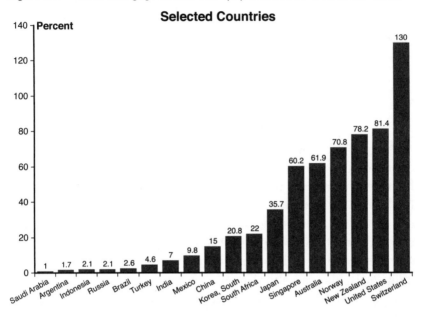

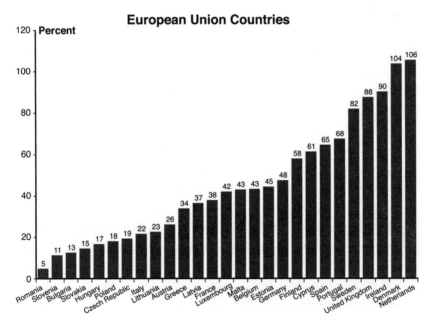

Note: Based on the latest available data. EMF Hypostat (2009) provides the latest data as of 2009, and Warnock and Warnock (2008) for the average data from 2001 to 2005.

Sources: EMF Hypostat (2009) for E.U. countries and Iceland, Russia, Norway, Turkey, and United States; Warnock and Warnock (2008) for the other countries.

Modern Housing Finance Takes Shape in the United States[8]

The financial system in a modern economy facilitates the transfer of resources from savers to borrowers. This allows the productive sectors to invest in capital necessary for growth. The financial system also allows consumers to adjust to variations in income over time, to smooth consumption. Homeownership, of course, requires financing, given the price of housing relative to the typical homeowners' income. The modern financing of housing largely began with the savings and loan industry in the United States.

Origin and Development of Savings and Loan Associations: The First Hundred Years (1830–1930)

The first American savings and loan (S&L) institution, the Oxford Provident Building Association, was founded in Frankford, Pennsylvania, on January 3, 1831. The association was organized to enable its member shareholders, most of whom were textile workers, to pool their savings so that a subset of them could obtain financing to build or buy homes. Every member was to be afforded the opportunity, over time, to borrow funds for this purpose, with the association terminating after the last member was accommodated. Association membership was geographically restricted: No loans were made for homes located more than 5 miles from Frankford.

This first savings and loan was organized as a mutual institution and therefore was owned by its shareholder members. New members were elected by ballot at shareholder meetings. Shareholders were expected to remain with the institution throughout its life, but those who wanted to withdraw their shares were allowed to do so if they gave a month's notice and paid a penalty of 5% of their withdrawal. The association's balance sheet consisted of mortgage loans as assets and ownership shares as liabilities, with relatively little net worth. These shares were the precursor of the savings deposits held today.[9]

The founders of the Frankford S&L envisioned an institution with a limited life in which the shareholders and the borrowers eventually became one and the same. The institution served the important role of consolidating the savings of a group of local individuals and rechanneling the funds to these same individuals in the form of mortgage loans.[10] Thus, the Frankford association filled a niche that was woefully underserviced by financial institutions at the time. Only much later did borrowers and savers become separate and distinct customers of these institutions.

Originally, institutions of this type were called building societies because they bought land and built homes. When they began lending to members to build their own homes, they were referred to as building and loan associations. After the 1930s, they tended to be called savings and loan associations, following the name given to the newly created federally chartered associations. Until the 1980s, all new federal associations had to begin as mutuals. With the passage of the Garn–St. Germain Depository Institutions Act of 1982, however, the federal regulator of these institutions, the Federal Home Loan Bank Board (FHLBB), could provide federal charters to new stock associations.

Perhaps it is not surprising that this financial need went largely unfulfilled by commercial and mutual savings banks.[11] These financial entities preceded the development of S&Ls, but neither catered to the home real estate market. Commercial banks issued liabilities consisting primarily of currency and demand deposits that were acceptable to their customers because they were meant to be backed by self-liquidating commercial loans. These banks catered to the short-term business loan market.

Mutual savings banks did not issue currency or accept demand deposits but were involved with the savings of the general public. Unlike savings and loans, however, they were originally philanthropic. Their intent was to provide financial services for the small saver, which required that their deposits be more flexible in terms of amounts and maturities and correspondingly required a much more flexible asset portfolio than just mortgages. Each type of institution specialized in a particular market, and the specialization was reflected in the balance sheets of these financial firms.

After the organization of the Frankford S&L, similar institutions spread throughout the United States—for example, entering New

York in 1836, South Carolina in 1843, and what is now Oklahoma in 1890. Accurate data on the number and assets of S&Ls before 1900 are not readily available. However, data for that year indicate that the total number of such institutions was 5,356, and total assets were $571 million. By 1930, before growth was interrupted by the Great Depression, the number of S&Ls had grown to nearly 12,000, and total assets were almost $9 billion.[12] S&L assets increased substantially as the number and income of shareholders grew.

As these associations spread throughout the country, innovations began to occur. For example, the self-terminating type of institution was replaced by a more permanent type, and the borrowers were separated from the savers. Thus, these firms began to operate with a long-term horizon in mind, and they began to accept shareholders who were not obliged to take out mortgage loans. This not only enlarged the pool of potential shareholders, but also emphasized the savings aspect of membership in an association. So the link between borrower and saver began to dissipate despite the mutual form of organization under which these firms usually operated. These institutions still generally did not take deposits, per se; in many states, in fact, they were precluded by law from doing so. Not until the advent of federal deposit insurance for savings and loans in the 1930s did the taking of deposits as such become widespread.[13]

Accompanying the growth of the savings and loan industry during its first century were state and eventually federal regulations. As the roles of saver and borrower became more distinct, and as the shareholders or owners became less directly involved in managing the associations, the public desire for monitoring and supervision grew. The state governments, which were the only chartering agents for the associations until the Great Depression, therefore became more involved with monitoring these early institutions.[14]

State supervision evolved from reports to officials, to permissive monitoring by regulators, and then to required periodic examinations.[15] In this way, states were able to show "their disapproval of loans for purposes not strictly within the building and loan field, which [was determined to be] the financing of single-family residences."[16]

In addition, "a rather common power given to the state official in charge of the supervision of building and loan associations [was] that of refusing to grant charters where there [did] not seem to be a necessity for another building and loan."[17] Thus, monitoring and supervision had three objectives: preventing and detecting fraud, limiting S&L lending to home loans, and curbing competition within the industry. This lenient regulation was fostered by the scarcity of reported failures of savings and loans in their formative years. However, failures increased during the economic downturn of the 1890s.

A major result of this downturn was the virtual elimination of the so-called national institutions. This type of institution developed in the 1880s by gathering deposits and making mortgage loans on a national scale through the use of branch offices and the mail. Although the downturn of the 1890s hit both nationally based and locally based institutions, local associations attributed their problems to the improper loan strategy and subsequent failures of the national institutions. They claimed that customers were unable to distinguish between the two types of firms during the panic of 1893. The increased competition engendered by the nationals also led to the establishment of the U.S. League of Local Building and Loan Associations. This group became very influential during the subsequent years and successfully lobbied the state legislatures to curb the activities of the national associations, a move that eventually drove the nationals out of business.[18]

Although the local savings and loans had effectively removed competition from the national associations, competition from commercial banks was beginning to develop. In the early 1900s, national banks were informed that they were not prohibited from accepting savings deposits. Moreover, Federal Reserve member banks were given an incentive to use this source of funds when a lower reserve requirement was placed on savings accounts than on demand deposits.

On the asset side, competition for residential mortgages was also beginning to develop between savings and loans and banks, albeit to a much lower degree. Without active secondary markets and with still somewhat restrictive regulations, the two types of depository institutions found that comparative advantages in information collection and processing, as well as the favorable tax treatment afforded savings and loans, still led to fairly identifiable balance sheet differences.

Thus, as the economic boom of the 1920s began, the banks and S&Ls maintained different balance sheets, competed only indirectly, and were regulated to a different degree and by different levels of government. The federal regulators were most interested in commercial banks and the payments mechanism, and the state governments were most directly involved with savings and loans and their role in facilitating homeownership.

It is interesting to note that, before World War II, noninstitutional sources were also major providers of home finance. Frederiksen (1984) reported that, in the late 1800s, about 55% of mortgages in the country were held by local investors who made the loans or sold the property themselves, and about 18% were held by nonresident investors. "[I]n America," he wrote, "the making of a mortgage loan is essentially a local transaction."

Frederiksen further noted that "it is entirely satisfactory only when the investor is personally familiar with the property mortgaged, and the insurance is kept up, and when, furthermore, he is able at any time to take steps to protect himself in case of default."

Frederiksen's study indicates that the mortgages averaged less than half of the value of the security and that less than half of the property in America was under mortgage.[19] Interestingly, when local investors were replaced increasingly by more formal and more regulated sources after World War II, two major real estate crises occurred, with the most recent one more widespread and costly than the earlier crisis.

As you can see in Table 2.1, S&Ls were a major provider of funding until 1980. Afterward, commercial banks became more important than S&Ls. But in recent decades, government-sponsored enterprises (GSEs) have dominated the field.

Table 2.1 Nonfarm Residential Mortgage Holdings, by Type of Institution[a] (1900–2010)

Year	Total Holdings (US$ Billions)	Percent of Total Holdings				
		CBs	S&Ls[b]	LICs	GSEs[c]	Other
1900	2.92	5.42	34.38	6.27	0.00	53.93
1905	3.52	8.32	36.08	7.22	0.00	48.38
1910	4.43	10.05	40.69	9.11	0.00	40.15
1915	6.01	9.41	41.82	8.68	0.00	40.09
1920	9.12	8.77	39.93	6.12	0.00	45.18
1925	17.23	10.78	40.80	8.17	0.00	40.24
1930	27.65	10.29	38.11	10.41	0.00	41.19
1935	22.21	10.02	32.80	9.91	0.00	47.28
1940	23.81	12.59	33.54	12.13	0.75	41.00
1945	24.64	13.78	34.69	14.74	0.03	36.77
1950	54.36	19.19	37.08	20.30	2.44	20.99
1960	162.11	12.56	49.77	17.73	1.79	18.14
1970	352.25	12.96	52.71	12.12	5.24	16.97
1975	574.64	14.43	53.62	6.48	11.11	14.35
1980	1,100.40	15.61	48.41	3.40	16.14	16.44
1985	1,732.10	13.60	37.58	1.94	28.15	18.74
1990	2,893.73	16.19	23.91	1.52	39.83	18.55
1995	3,719.23	18.63	14.64	1.05	48.35	17.34
2000	5,508.59	19.02	11.90	0.75	49.49	18.85
2005	10,049.21	19.21	10.47	0.50	40.74	29.08
2010	11,386.53	21.11	4.32	0.46	53.77	20.33

[a] Commercial banks (CBs), savings and loans (S&Ls), life insurance companies (LICs), government-sponsored enterprises (GSEs), and "other," which includes state and local government employee retirement funds, private issuers of asset-backed securities, finance companies, real estate investment trusts, and credit unions.

[b] Includes mutual savings banks (MSBs).

[c] This number includes all government-sponsored institutions participating in the mortgage market (government-sponsored enterprises and agency- and GSE-backed mortgage pools), both on-balance sheet holdings and securitized mortgages.

Sources: U.S. Federal Reserve Flow of Funds and Bureau of the Census, *Statistical Abstract Supplement, Historical Statistics of the United States*, 1961.

As shown in Figure 2.3, financing of homeownership differs substantially across countries. In the U.S., securitization has clearly become important, whereas in Denmark, covered bonds dominate.

In other countries, such as Australia, Japan, Austria, Finland, France, Germany, and Greece, homeownership has been financed largely through the use of deposits at financial institutions.

Figure 2.3   Sources of funding for home mortgages in selected countries, 2009.

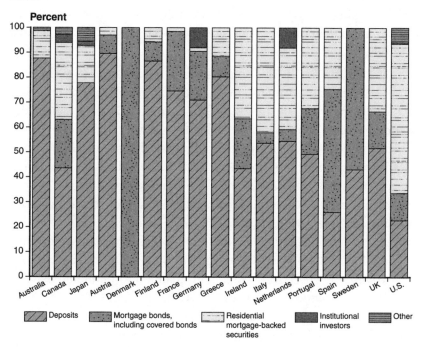

Note: Based on the latest available data from the following sources.

Sources: Author's calculation. U.S. Federal Reserve Flow of Funds (2009) for the United States; Hypostat (2009) for E.U. countries; Odaira and Takado (2008) and Japan's Government Housing Loan Corporation; and Australian Bureau of Statistics.

Savings and Loan Associations and the Great Depression

There have been only two periods in the first 150 years of savings and loan history in which the institutions suffered large-scale failures. The first was the severe economic downturn of the 1890s, and the second was the Great Depression of the 1930s.

During the Great Depression, savings and loans did not accept demand deposits and, therefore, did not suffer the runs that reportedly plagued commercial banks. Nevertheless, their members had to draw upon their savings to maintain consumption. S&Ls were hard pressed to cope with these withdrawals because their assets were almost entirely mortgages, and they prided themselves on maintaining low liquidity levels. Moreover, reserves for losses were relatively low because "many state laws...discouraged the accumulation of reserves and some supervisory authorities practically forced the distribution of all earnings."[20] As withdrawals mounted and assets declined in value due to delinquencies and defaults, S&Ls failed. These failures severely limited the flow of funds to housing.[21]

This disruption in the housing market finally changed the role of the federal government in the regulation of the savings and loan industry. First, on July 22, 1932, President Hoover signed the Federal Home Loan Bank Act. This act set up the Federal Home Loan Bank System, consisting of 12 regional Federal Home Loan (FHL) banks under the supervision of the Federal Home Loan Bank Board (FHLBB) in Washington. The main purpose of the system was to financially strengthen member savings and loan associations by providing them with an alternative and steady source of funds for promoting homeownership.[22] Member savings and loan associations included all federal associations and any state-chartered institutions that voluntarily chose to become and qualified to be members. The system was designed so that the FHL Banks could issue bonds in the capital markets and thus be able to provide advances to healthy and reasonably safe institutions. It was not intended to bail out failing thrifts.[23]

Second, the Home Owners' Loan Act was signed June 13, 1933. Although the main purpose of the act was to facilitate the refinancing of existing mortgages in distress cases, many borrowers seeking the more favorable interest rate and other terms the government offered were also able to obtain loans. This led many borrowers to deliberately default on their existing loans, thus exacerbating the problems of the S&Ls.[24] (Amid the mortgage market meltdown from 2007 to 2010, some Americans may also have had an incentive to default on loans, due to favorable government support or an inability of private lenders to seek adequate legal recourse against defaulters.)[25]

Another purpose of the 1933 act was to allow the Federal Home Loan Bank Board to charter federal savings and loans. This was not an attempt to drive the state-chartered institutions out of business. Instead, the aim was to establish S&Ls in places where the state institutions were providing insufficient service. Furthermore, the federal S&Ls were to be mutual-type associations and to operate only in the local areas where they were chartered.[26]

Finally, Title IV of the National Housing Act, enacted June 27, 1934, created the Federal Savings and Loan Insurance Corporation (FSLIC) to provide deposit insurance for savings deposits at savings and loans. Membership in the FSLIC was made compulsory for federal associations and optional for state-chartered associations. With the establishment of the FSLIC, the savings and loans were placed on equal footing with commercial banks, which were insured by the Federal Deposit Insurance Corporation (FDIC). Eventually, the FDIC became the administrator of the federal deposit insurance fund for savings and loans as well.

Postwar Growth and Diversification in the Savings and Loan Industry

Following the Great Depression and World War II, savings and loans experienced tremendous growth for close to four decades. They surpassed mutual savings banks in terms of total assets for the first time in 1954 and grew to half the size of the commercial banking industry by the end of 1980. This expansion was spread throughout the entire industry, with large and small institutions participating.

The magnitude of the redistribution is remarkable. Private financial assets in 1945 totaled $247 billion. Of this amount, savings and loan associations held a meager 3%, compared to 65% for commercial banks. By 1975, however, savings and loans had increased their share of the total to 16%, while the share for commercial banks had dropped to 37%. Mutual savings banks and life insurance companies also lost considerable ground during this period.

Moreover, although the share of total financial assets accounted for by all the depository financial services firms declined to 51% from 76%, the share of S&Ls quintupled. The relative growth in S&Ls is even more impressive in light of the increased competition among financial institutions.

In the 1950s and 1960s, more than half of the deposits in commercial banks were noninterest-bearing checking accounts or demand deposits (which savings and loans did not offer). However, by the late 1970s, demand deposits made up only about one-fourth of commercial bank deposits. At savings and loans over this same period, time and passbook savings accounts remained about the same, 75% to 80% of total deposits, and S&Ls offered virtually no transactions accounts. The commercial banks were therefore beginning to compete more directly for the saver's dollar, but savings and loans had not yet received unrestricted permission to compete for the commercial banks' bread-and-butter accounts.

In addition to facing competition from other depository institutions, some nondepository financial institutions were being developed to help small savers combat the ravages inflicted on their portfolios by inflation and high interest rates. Laws and regulations generally prohibited savings and loans and other depository institutions from paying interest on checking deposits and limited the rates of interest and maturities on savings and time deposits. As a result, customers of these institutions increasingly began to go to the relatively unregulated nondepository financial firms in search of higher interest rates.

This interaction between market interest rates and regulatory constraints led to the development of money market mutual funds. These funds attracted customers by offering a new type of account. Not being subject to depository institution regulations, this account offered higher rates of interest than other financial depository service firms could pay, and it included limited check-writing privileges.

By the late 1970s, these money market funds, which had been introduced in 1972, had grown large enough to be a serious competitive threat to depository financial institutions. This threat spurred the development and regulatory approval of new market-based accounts offered by depository institutions, such as the money market certificate in 1978, whose rate was tied to the six-month Treasury bill rate.

Although the 1970s marked the beginning of what became extensive changes on the liability side of the depository institutions' balance sheet, not until the 1980s did the asset side catch up with the changes.

Congress rejected variable-rate mortgages, which existed in the early 1970s in some states, such as Wisconsin and California, on a national basis in 1974. Although federally chartered savings and loans were allowed to issue variable-rate mortgages in states where state-chartered institutions were permitted to do so, not until January 1, 1979, were all federally chartered S&Ls allowed to offer variable-rate, graduated-payment, and reverse-annuity mortgages on a national basis.

Tax law in the savings and loan industry came into play in 1951. Before the Revenue Act of 1951, savings and loans were exempt from federal income taxes. Although this act terminated their tax-exempt status, savings and loans nonetheless were able to avoid paying taxes because they were permitted to essentially deduct up to 100% of taxable income through a bad-debt reserve.

In 1962, however, another Revenue Act was passed that reduced the bad-debt deduction to 60% of taxable income, subject to a qualifying asset restriction. This restriction stated that, for a savings and loan to be eligible for the maximum deduction, 82% or more of its assets had to consist of cash, U.S. government securities, and passbook loans, plus one-to-four family residential property loans. The deduction was zero if these assets fell below 60%. The Tax Reform Act of 1969 modified this restriction by permitting a savings and loan association to base its bad-debt deduction on taxable income, loss experience, or percentage of eligible loans.

Because the vast majority of associations used the taxable-income method, the deduction was reduced in scheduled steps from 60% of taxable income in 1969 to 40% in 1979.[27] The Tax Equity and Fiscal Responsibility Act of 1982 further reduced the bad-debt deduction to 34% in 1982 and then to 32% in 1984. The Tax Reform Act of 1986 reduced the bad-debt deduction as a percent of taxable income to 8% in 1987. Thus, over time, the tax laws have provided a large but diminishing incentive to invest in eligible mortgage-related assets.

In addition to the tax laws, regulations pertained to FHLBB member associations, FSLIC-insured associations, federal associations, and state associations. The Interest Rate Control Act of 1966, for example, gave the FHLBB the authority to set rate ceilings, which until then had been nonexistent, on the savings deposits of member associations. This ceiling was set initially at one-half of 1% but later was reduced to one-fourth of 1%, above the ceiling rate that commercial banks were permitted to pay on savings deposits. The ceiling represented an attempt to provide a competitive edge to savings and loans to garner funds for the residential housing sector. This differential was abolished in January 1984, and all rate ceilings for depository institutions were eliminated in March 1986.

The regulations for federal associations were initially quite direct in their intention to limit lending to local home mortgage loans, which meant loans secured by houses within 50 miles of the association's home office.

In 1964, federal associations were permitted to make unsecured personal loans for college or educational expenses, the first time they had been allowed to make loans for any purpose other than acquiring real estate. In the same year, the geographical limit for mortgage loans was extended to 100 miles. Congress later extended this limit to encompass the association's home state—and beyond that for the largest savings and loans. Then in 1983, the FHLBB permitted federal associations to make loans nationwide. Unless prohibited by state law, state associations with FSLIC insurance were permitted to do the same. In 100 years, the savings and loan industry had come full circle—nationals were once again alive and well.[28]

Federal associations were also permitted in 1964 to issue mortgages and buy property in urban renewal areas and to buy securities issued by federal, state, and municipal governments. In 1968, these associations were allowed to make loans for mobile homes, second or vacation homes, and housing fixtures. Thus began the entry by savings and loans into business areas long viewed as the exclusive domain of commercial banks.

Turbulent 1980s for the Savings and Loan Industry

As interest rates rose unexpectedly and fluctuated widely in the late 1970s and early 1980s, it became clear that many savings and loans were ill equipped to handle the new financial environment. Their newly authorized market-rate deposits were rapidly escalating the institutions' cost of funds, while the largely fixed-rate mortgage portfolios were painfully slow to turn over.

The result was rapidly deteriorating profits and a significant increase in failures. The problems persisted—even as interest rates declined in 1982 and the maturity-mismatch problem lessened— due to a growing deterioration in the quality of assets held by many associations.

The savings and loan industry's ratio of net worth to total assets fell from more than 5% at the end of 1979 to 3.4% at the end of 1985. During this same period, more than 500 savings and loans failed and an additional 400 or so were left with negative net worth. By the end of the decade, approximately 500 more associations had failed and the government had bailed out the industry. A few years later, the insurance fund for savings and loans was merged into the insurance fund for commercial banks.

The turbulence of the early 1980s, however, did more than reduce the number of institutions. It permanently affected the way savings and loans were to do business. Instead of offering just savings and time deposits, these institutions began to offer transaction accounts, large certificates of deposit, and consumer repurchase agreements— virtually as wide a selection as that of any commercial bank. On the asset side, these institutions went beyond mortgages to hold consumer loans, commercial loans, mortgage-backed securities, and a wide variety of direct investments. From then on, savings and loans differed from commercial banks more as a matter of degree than of kind.[29] The distinctions among the depository financial services firms became forever blurred.

Federal Government Involvement in Mortgage Markets[30]

The initial spread of home mortgages came after the National Banking Act in 1863, which enabled an expansion of bank charters and greater lending. Mortgage insurance helped smooth the way for credit that fueled homebuilding. The idea of a guarantee was later extended to municipal bonds, which furthered infrastructure financing that created the framework for further residential expansion. Mortgage insurance later expanded throughout the twentieth century (see Table 2.3 later in the chapter).

Since the 1930s, the federal government has played an increasingly important role in the allocation of mortgage credit. Instruments of federal policy used for this purpose include or have included loans insured and guaranteed by the Federal Housing Administration and Veterans Administration; secondary mortgage transactions by the Federal National Mortgage Association, Federal Home Loan Mortgage Corporation, and Government National Mortgage Association; interest rate subsidies; tax expenditures; and direct loans. Federal regulations have been enacted to affect the behavior of mortgage lenders in the pursuit of social objectives. These regulations include the Fair Housing Act (Title VIII), the Equal Credit Opportunity Act, the Home Mortgage Disclosure Act, and the Community Reinvestment Act.

Housing policies are clearly a part of the stabilization, allocation, and distribution activities of the federal government. The first major federal housing initiatives, enacted in the National Housing Act of 1934, as mentioned earlier, were part of an economic recovery program implemented during the Great Depression. Though stabilization of economic activity has remained an important objective, allocation and distribution objectives have become increasingly important. Indeed, the 1949 Housing Act explicitly acknowledged such aims, proposing a "goal of a decent home and a suitable living environment for every American family."

An implicit but important goal of federal housing policies has been to encourage the acceptance of greater risk in mortgage markets. Encouraging greater risk taking may be socially desirable for reasons of economic efficiency and distributional equity. However, attitudes toward risk by private lenders and federal, state, and local financial regulatory agencies may prevent mortgage transactions that would be profitable for borrowers and lenders. In such cases, appropriately designed federal mortgage insurance programs may enhance the efficiency of mortgage markets. For numerous reasons, low-income applicants for mortgages are likely to be more risky. Improving the access of such individuals or groups to mortgage credit through government actions can be a means of achieving greater distributional equity.

Table 2.2 shows that the United States is one of relatively few countries among those listed in which the government provides support to residential mortgage markets.[31] As a result of the recent mortgage market meltdown in the United States, the role of the government in mortgage markets has been reconsidered. However, as of the writing of this book, no legislative action had been taken to make any major changes.

Table 2.2   Government Mortgage Market Support

Country	Government Mortgage Insurer	Government Security Guarantees	Government-Sponsored Enterprises
Denmark	No	No	No
Germany	No	No	No
Ireland	No	No	No
Netherlands	NHG	No	No
Spain	No	No	No
U.K.	No	No	No
Australia	No	No	No
Canada	Canada Mortgage Housing Corporation	Canada Mortgage Housing Corporation	No
Japan	No	Japan Housing Finance Agency	Possible
South Korea	No	No	Korean Housing Finance Corporation
Switzerland	No	No	No
U.S.	FHA	GNMA	Fannie Mae, Freddie Mac, FHLBs

Source: Michael Lea, *International Comparison of Mortgage Product Offerings,* Special Report, Research Institute for Housing America, Mortgage Banker Association, September 2010.

It should also be noted that the Canada Mortgage and Housing Corporation, which is a 100% government-owned and -controlled corporation, insures (guarantees) mortgage loans and securitizes some of the insured loans. Pollock points out that CMHC is "in one sense…a combination of FHA and Ginnie Mae." He adds that it insures roughly half of Canadian mortgages, which is the same proportion as the combined Fannie Mae and Freddie Mac in the United States.[32] Homeownership rates are nearly identical in the two countries, as shown in earlier Figure 2.1.

Furthermore, despite all the U.S. government support for homeownership, Australia, Ireland, Spain, and the United Kingdom all have higher homeownership rates with far less government support.

Development and Impact of Government and Private Insurance for Home Mortgages[33]

The first private mortgage insurance company was established in Rochester, New York, in 1887.[34] During the 1920s, the U.S. mortgage market relied heavily on mutual savings banks, savings and loan associations, insurance companies, and commercial banks. These four types of institutions accounted for 74.4% of the total new mortgage loans made on one- to four-family houses from 1925 to 1930.[35]

The typical mortgage terms on loans these institutions made during this period were quite different from those prevailing in subsequent periods, including the present. During the 1920s, mortgages were written with the term to maturity not exceeding 12 years and with loan-to-value ratios close to 50%. In the 1930s and 1940s, however, these mortgage terms were significantly liberalized. By 1947, the term to maturity approached 20 years and the loan-to-value ratio was roughly 70%. In more recent years, both of these factors were further liberalized.

During the 1930s, the housing and banking industries virtually collapsed. In 1930–1933, more than 8,800 banks failed. In 1933 alone, 3,891 banks suspended operations.[36] Total housing starts fell 70%, from 2,383,000 in 1926–1930 to 728,000 in 1931–1935. It is estimated that only 150,000 persons were employed in on-site construction in 1933.[37]

At the same time, approximately half of all home mortgages were in default, and foreclosures were occurring at the phenomenal rate of more than 1,000 per day.[38] Nonfarm real estate foreclosures reached a maximum of 252,000 in 1933. Foreclosures declined only slightly at first, to 229,000 in 1935, but then declined more rapidly to 185,000 in 1936, 151,000 in 1937, and 59,000 in 1941.[39]

Among the responses of the federal government to these events were the establishment of the Home Owner's Loan Corporation (HOLC) in 1933 and the passage of the National Housing Act of 1934, which created the FHA mortgage insurance programs.

HOLC was established to buy mortgages in default and threatened with foreclosure. It was therefore directly concerned with mortgage debt and only indirectly, if at all, with the availability of new mortgage credit. At its peak in 1935, HOLC held more than 15% of all U.S. residential mortgage debt. HOLC was expected to incur large losses as a result of its activities—primarily the extension of emergency loans on a long-term, self-amortizing basis. However, when liquidated in the 1940s, HOLC fully repaid all its Treasury borrowings and actually showed a small profit.

By contrast, the National Housing Act of 1934 was designed to increase the availability of new mortgage credit and thereby encourage the revival of the housing industry. The principal instrument was Section 203(b) of the National Housing Act. (Since the passage of this Act, new FHA mortgage programs have been implemented as amendments to this act and are commonly known by their section number and letter.)

Mortgages insured under Section 203(b) were secured by the Mutual Mortgage Insurance Fund (MMIF). The creation of the

Federal National Mortgage Association (FNMA, also known as Fannie Mae) in 1938 provided additional impetus to 203(b) mortgage activity because FNMA was authorized to buy such mortgages. FNMA therefore made FHA mortgages extremely liquid by providing a ready secondary market for the longer-term type of mortgages offered under Section 203(b).

The main feature of Section 203(b) was the provision of mortgage insurance to all borrowers at a uniform premium. Each 203(b) loan was to be evaluated on the basis of economic soundness to ensure the solvency of the MMIF. Though no formal definition of economic soundness was provided in the legislation, limits were placed on the maximum mortgage amount and the maximum loan-to-value ratio. However, general consensus in the literature states that FHA implemented Section 203(b) mortgage insurance by imposing minimum values on neighborhood quality, property quality, and borrowers' credit worthiness. These criteria were implemented by conducting a property inspection, and maximum permissible values were established for monthly payment-to-income ratios. Furthermore, the actual operation of the Section 203(b) program indicated that some urban areas were excluded from FHA insurance. This practice of exclusion was characterized as "redlining" because excluded areas were said to be marked by a red line at FHA offices.

High levels of mortgage insurance activity experienced under Section 203(b) during the 1930s, 1940s, and 1950s, along with sizable surpluses in the MMIF, indicate that, during this period, the bulk of FHA-insured mortgage loans were profitable. Indeed, as early as 1938, the maximum loan amount and the maximum loan-to-value ratio were increased based on favorable loss experience. Subsequently, these maximums were further increased. Government insurance transactions generally met or exceeded the criterion of actuarial or economic soundness. Note, however, that it is possible for the average transaction to earn a profit even though the marginal loan transaction, at the highest loan-to-value ratio, may suffer a loss.

The U.S. Congress has traditionally set the maximum mortgage amount that can be insured under FHA programs. In 2008, under the basic Section 203(b) single-family mortgage insurance program, the limit was $362,790. Thirty years earlier, in 1978, the limit was $60,000, which was in force since 1977. Before then, the cap was $45,000, a limit introduced by the Housing and Community Development Act of 1974. Until the passage of this act, the mortgage limit was $33,000.

If housing prices rise more rapidly than these congressionally determined mortgage limits, the maximum permissible loan-to-value ratios must necessarily fall. This reduction in the real value of mortgage limits in inflationary periods induces borrowers to shift to conventional mortgage loans.[40]

The 1950s also saw the revival of the private mortgage insurance (PMI) industry, which began to offer insurance for conventional mortgage loans for the first time since the 1930s.[41] The industry had collapsed during the Great Depression.[42] As the result of legislation passed in 1956 in Wisconsin, the Mortgage Guarantee Insurance Corporation began operating in 1957. Subsequently, more PMIs were permitted to operate as additional states passed enabling legislation permitting this kind of insurance.

The PMIs became increasingly important in the mortgage insurance market thereafter. The standard mortgage insurance policy indemnifies the beneficiary against losses in the event of default, with the amount indemnified depending on the special coverage chosen.[43]

An increase in the demand for conventional loans, of course, also results in an increase in the demand for PMI.[44] When the U.S. housing market collapsed in 2007 and 2008, mortgage insurers paid $15 billion in claims.[45]

PMI competes with FHA insurance by offering lower premiums for safer mortgages. FHA generally sets an insurance premium of 0.5% of the outstanding mortgage amount, collected over the life of the loan on a current basis, on all its loans. In contrast, PMI premiums vary according to the loan-to-value ratio of the mortgage, the percentage of the mortgage amount insured, and the choice of prepayment option with fixed length of coverage.

Of course, these premiums are set lower than the FHA premium because the PMI companies insure only relatively low-risk mortgage loans, a practice known as "cream skimming." FHA is left with the rest. However, the FHA demonstrated positive profits associated with higher loan-to-value mortgages that were not being exploited by conventional mortgage lenders. Increased PMI activity decreases the volume of Section 203(b) insurance activity and raises the loss rate, thereby reducing the surplus in the MMIF. Both of these outcomes have been observed.

This does not mean, however, that the FHA mortgage insurance program has necessarily been a failure. The FHA has made a number of important contributions, including assisting in popularizing and standardizing the fully amortized, fixed-interest, level-payment mortgage; lengthening the term of the mortgage; increasing the loan-to-value ratios on residential mortgages; developing minimum property standards, standardized appraisals, and the standardization of the mortgage contract; and providing information on risks of default that was then available to private mortgage lenders and insurers. All these factors, of course, have contributed to the development of a truly national mortgage market. Furthermore, the FHA thus far has never requested an appropriation for MMIF.[46]

The accomplishments should not, however, be overstated. The surplus in the MMIF in earlier years may have demonstrated to private mortgage lenders that relatively high loan-to-value ratios were potentially profitable. It is uncertain, however, whether private lenders could have increased their loan-to-value ratios before the introduction of FHA mortgage insurance. In this regard, Leo Grebler states:

The restrictions on loan-to-value ratios and maturity of mort-gage loans imposed by the National Banking Act do not apply to loans insured by the Federal Housing Administration or guaranteed by the Veterans Administration. This is also true for the limitations in many of the state banking laws. While similar exceptions apply to other mortgage lending institu-tions, they are more potent in the case of commercial banks because their conventional lending activity is more severely limited by existing laws.[47]

This quotation suggests that private lenders making conventional mortgage loans may have been unable in earlier years to liberalize their loan terms because of federal, state, and/or local regulations and laws. Over time, as these regulations and laws were liberalized, lenders' offer curves shifted upward to take advantage of opportunities flowing from the ability to lend on less restrictive terms. The recent housing problems in the United States indicate what happens when loan terms become too lenient.

The introduction of PMI encouraged lenders to make larger loans because, with insurance, conventional loans could be sold to such institutions as FNMA and FHLMC (discussed in the next section). Until these institutions were created or were permitted to buy conventional insured mortgages, however, lenders were undoubtedly reluctant to liberalize their loan terms, particularly when faced with usury laws or "soundness" requirements imposed by federal or state regulatory agencies.

Table 2.3 shows that mortgage insurance is available in many other countries. The insurance is offered by the private sector, as well as by government entities.

Table 2.3 Mortgage Insurance Timeline

Year	Country	Sponsorship/Event
1887	United States	First private mortgage insurance company started in New York.
1904	United States	First law on mortgage insurance passed in New York.
1934	United States	Federal sponsorship
1950	The Philippines	Public sponsorship
1954	Canada	Public sponsorship
1956	United States	First post-Depression private mortgage insurance company chartered in Wisconsin.
1957	Netherlands	Public–private combination
1961	Guatemala	Public sponsorship
1963	Canada	Private sponsorship
1965	Australia	Private sponsorship
Pre-1970	United Kingdom	Private sponsorship
1987	United States	State sponsorship
1989	South Africa	NGO/private reinsurance
1992	Sweden	Public and private sponsorship

Sponsorship type	Country	Year
Public sponsorship	Finland	Mid-1990s
Public–private combination	Mali	1998
Private sponsorship	Ireland	1998
Public sponsorship	Peru	1999
Public sponsorship	West Bank and Gaza	2000
Private sponsorship	Portugal	2003
Public sponsorship	Kazakhstan	2004
Public sponsorship2	Morocco	2004

Year	Country	Sponsorship type
1993	France	Public–private combination
1997	New Zealand	Public sponsorship
1998	Israel	Private sponsorship
1999	Hong Kong	Public–private reinsurance
1999	Lithuania	Public sponsorship
2000	Algeria	Public sponsorship
2002	Spain	Private sponsorship
2003	Italy	Private sponsorship
2004	Colombia	Public sponsorship
2004	Mexico	Public sponsorship
2007	New Zealand	Private sponsorship
2007	Mexico	Private sponsorship

Sources: Loïc Chiquier and Michael Lea. *Housing Finance Policy in Emerging Market*, 2009; Dwight Jaffee, *Monoline Restrictions, with Applications to Mortgage Insurance and Title Insurance*, 2006; and www.soa.org/library/monographs/finance/housing-wealth/2009/september/mono-2009-mfi09-herzog-history.pdf.

The Golden Age of Government-Sponsored Enterprises (GSEs)[48]

The U.S. established several government-sponsored institutions to support the housing sector (see Table 2.4).

Table 2.4 Housing Government-Sponsored Enterprises

Organization	Known As	Established Date	Purpose, Function, and Current Status
Federal Home Loan Banks	FHLBs	1932	FHLBs are a network of 12 regional banks that provide stable, low-cost funding to financial institutions for home mortgages; small business loans; and rural, agricultural, and economic development lending. The FHL Banks are the largest source of home mortgage and community credit in the United States, providing funding to other banks, though not directly to individual borrowers. Thousands of member institutions hold equity stakes in the FHL Banks.
Federal National Mortgage Association	Fannie Mae	1938	Fannie Mae is a publicly traded corporation founded during the Great Depression. In 1968, it was chartered by Congress as a government-sponsored enterprise. Fannie Mae does not directly issue home loans, but operates in the secondary mortgage market, buying and guaranteeing conforming loans. Its presence provides liquidity to mortgage originators, freeing up funds for mortgage companies, savings and loans, commercial banks, credit unions, and state and local housing finance agencies to increase lending to greater numbers of homebuyers. Fannie Mae and Freddie Mac held or backed half of the $12 trillion U.S. mortgage market in 2008. After sustaining huge losses, the two GSEs were placed in conservatorship in September 2008, under the supervision of the Federal Housing Finance Agency.

Government National Mortgage Association	Ginnie Mae	1968	Ginnie Mae is a U.S. government–owned corporation overseen by the Department of Housing and Urban Development. Ginnie Mae guarantees securities backed by federally insured loans, including those guaranteed by the FHA and VA. These are the only mortgage-backed securities guaranteed by the federal government.
Federal Home Loan Mortgage Corporation	Freddie Mac	1970	Freddie Mac was created to expand the secondary market for mortgages in the U.S. This publicly traded corporation and government-sponsored enterprise buys and guarantees conforming mortgage loans, pools them, and sells them to investors as mortgage-backed securities, providing liquidity to lenders. In September 2008, federal regulators took over Freddie Mac and Fannie Mae, placing both GSEs under the conservatorship of the Federal Housing Finance Agency.

Source: Barth, et al., *The Rise and Fall of the U.S. Mortgage and Credit Markets: A Comprehensive Analysis of the Meltdown* (Hoboken: John Wiley & Sons, 2009).

First, as noted earlier, the Federal Home Loan Bank Act set up the Federal Home Loan Bank System in 1932, consisting of 12 regional Federal Home Loan Banks under the supervision of the FHLBB in Washington. Its main purpose was to financially strengthen member savings and loans by providing them with an alternative and steady source of funds to promote homeownership. It now provides such funding to all depository institutions.

Second, the FNMA was established in 1938 to buy home mortgages and thereby created a secondary market for such mortgages.

Third, the Federal Home Loan Mortgage Corporation (FHLMC, also known as Freddie Mac) was established in 1970 to increase the availability of residential mortgage credit by contributing to the development and maintenance of the secondary market for residential mortgages.

Because the FHLMC primarily buys conventional mortgages and then issues securities backed by those mortgages, a process known as securitization, its creation increased the liquidity of this type of mortgage loan. More important, however, is the FHLMC policy (required by its enabling legislation) of limiting its purchases of conventional mortgages to those in which the borrower has at least 20% equity in the property or in which a lower borrower equity is accompanied by private mortgage insurance so that the effective exposure risk is reduced to 80% of the loan amount. Clearly, this policy increased the demand for PMI. About the same time that the FHLMC was created, the Emergency Home Loan Financing Act of 1970 authorized the FNMA to buy conventional mortgages and also securitize home mortgages.

The Federal Housing Enterprises Financial Safety and Soundness Act of 1992 established goals for Fannie Mae and Freddie Mac for financing affordable housing and housing in inner cities and rural and other undeserved markets. In 1996, the affordable housing goal was increased from 40% to 42% of their financing to go to borrowers with low and moderate incomes for each year from 1997 through 2000. This goal was boosted to 50% for the years 2001–2004 and raised still higher, as shown in Table 2.5.

Table 2.5 Housing Goals Set for Fannie Mae and Freddie Mac

	1997–2000 Housing Goals	2001–2004 Housing Goals	2005–2008 Housing Goals			
			2005	2006	2007	2008
Low and moderate income	42%	50%	52%	53%	55%	56%
Underserved areas	24%	31%	37%	38%	38%	39%
Special affordable housing	14%	20%	22%	23%	25%	27%

Sources: Federal Register, Milken Institute.

There are also goals for underserved areas (low-income and/or high-minority census tracts and rural counties) and special affordable housing (very low-income families and low-income families living in low-income areas.)

Figure 2.4a shows the ratio of total mortgages outstanding to GDP over the past century. Figure 2.4b shows the growing importance of financial institutions such as the FHLMC and FNMA in financing home ownership over the past three decades. (As a result of the mortgage market meltdown, however, their future remains uncertain as of the writing of this book.) Similar to the FHLMC, the FNMA can buy high loan-to-value ratio conventional loans only if these loans have private mortgage insurance. FNMA activities and policies therefore also increased the demand for PMI.[49] In the early 1970s, regulations were also promulgated permitting thrift institutions to originate mortgages at 95% of value when the individual loans are insured.

The securitization of residential mortgages has clearly spread beyond the United States during the past 30 years, as shown in Table 2.6. Other developments have also facilitated the financing of homeownership, such as covered bonds in Denmark and Pfandbrief in Germany. Clearly, however, the use of securitization and covered bonds to fund home purchases is found in more mature economies due to their more complex legal and financial issues.

Figure 2.4a   Total mortgages outstanding as percentage of GDP.

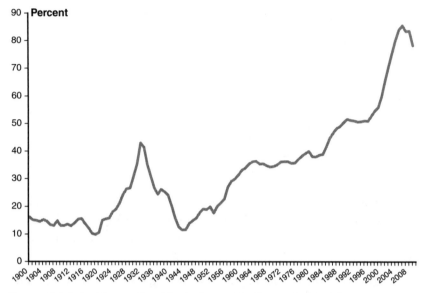

Sources: U.S. Federal Reserve Flow of Funds, Bureau of the Census, *Statistical Abstract Supplement, Historical Statistics of the United States*, 1961; and Bureau of Economic Analysis.

Figure 2.4b   Total home mortgages outstanding and share of home financing provided by government-sponsored enterprises.

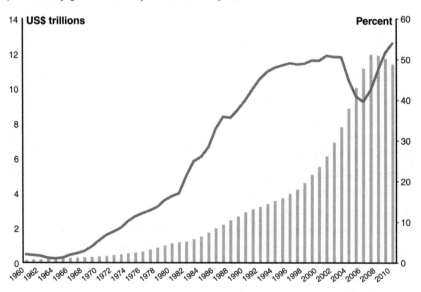

Sources: U.S. Federal Reserve Flow of Funds, Bureau of the Census, *Statistical Abstract Supplement, Historical Statistics of the United States,* 1961; and Bureau of Economic Analysis.

Table 2.6 Mortgage-Backed Securitization Timeline

Event	Country	Year	Year	Country	Event
First mortgage-backed securitization	United States	1970	1975	United States	First derivative on mortgage-backed securities
First mortgage-backed securitization	Australia	1984	1984	Canada	First mortgage securitization
First mortgage-backed securitization	United Kingdom	1985	1988	France	First mortgage-backed securitization
First mortgage-backed securitization	South Africa	1989	1991	Spain	First mortgage-backed securitization
First mortgage-backed securitization	Germany	1995	1995	Ireland	First mortgage-backed securitization
First mortgage-backed securitization	Argentina	1996			
First mortgage-backed securitization (CRI)	Brazil	1999	1999	Japan	First mortgage-backed securitization
First mortgage-backed securitization	Italy			South Korea	First mortgage-backed securitization
First mortgage-backed securitization	India	2000	2003	Mexico	First mortgage-backed securitization
First mortgage-backed securitization	Malaysia	2004	2005	China	First securitization of residential mortgages
First mortgage-backed securitization	Russia	2006	2006	Saudi Arabia	First mortgage-backed securitization in Gulf Cooperation Council (GCC) countries

Source: Milken Institute, Capital Access Index, 2005.

Federal Policies to Address Special Housing Problems in Inner Cities[50]

In the 1950s and 1960s, federal housing policy focused increasingly on inner cities. This represented a basic shift from the primary emphasis placed in the 1930s and 1940s on increasing the supply of adequate housing. This change was initially reflected in the Omnibus Housing Act of 1954, which, under Section 220, attempted to expand housing credit and production in urban renewal areas and, under Section 221(d)(2), provided mortgage insurance to families displaced by urban renewal. This legislation referred to the unmet goals of the National Housing Act of 1949 as the primary mandate for policy rather than revival of the housing industry or the financial system.

In addition, the Federal National Mortgage Charter Act of 1954 established the first special assistance functions (which require governmental financial support) to be carried out by the FNMA. These new programs were established with their own statutory provisions and insurance funds to permit them to function almost independently of the FHA. This was done to insulate the original FHA mortgage insurance fund, supporting programs such as Section 203 single-family home mortgage insurance from the effects of the relatively liberal underwriting terms of each new program.

Liberalization of mortgage terms relative to those in effect for the regular government mortgage insurance programs was a major feature of the 1954 Housing Act and the 1954 Mortgage Charter Act. This liberalization was basically achieved in three different ways. First, the "economic soundness" test for the proposed construction was replaced with an "acceptable risk" test, which required that the property to be insured meet "such standards and conditions as the Secretary shall prescribe to establish the acceptability of such property for insurance under this section." Second, the maximum insurable mortgage loan was based on "replacement cost" rather than the more conservative estimate of long-range "value." Third, the maximum allowable ratio of loan to "replacement cost" was increased. In some cases, the maximum term of the mortgage was also lengthened, thereby permitting lower monthly payments.

The trend toward liberalization continued with the enactment of Sections 231 and 202 in the Housing Act of 1959 and with the Housing Act of 1961. Section 231 in the 1959 act provided for generous insurance terms on housing for the elderly. In addition, Section 202 provided loans at subsidized interest rates to developers of private housing for the elderly.

The 1961 Housing Act further relaxed the terms of government mortgage insurance and broadened the coverage of Section 221(d)(2) insurance to include low- and moderate- income families. This section enabled such families to acquire housing at low down payments.

The 1961 Housing Act provided for subsidized, below-market interest rate (BMIR) mortgage insurance. The relevant section is 221(d)(3), which allowed loans at low interest rates to nonprofit or limited dividend corporations or cooperatives for the construction of modest housing for moderate-income households. Section 221(d)(3) is nominally structured as an interest subsidy program. However, lenders made such loans only because FNMA (later GNMA) immediately bought the BMIR mortgage at par, meaning FMNA (GNMA) was the actual lender. Hence, Section 221(d)(3) incorporated elements of a public interest subsidy and a direct loan program. Through the provisions of Section 221 (d)(3), the 1961 Housing Act reduced the reliance on mortgage insurance in government housing policy.

The one exception to this tendency was the previously described expansion of mortgage insurance under Section 221(d)(2). However, the mid-1960s saw a renewed emphasis on the role of federal mortgage guarantee programs in encouraging private lending in declining inner-city areas. This was undoubtedly due in part to the tendency of the FHA to follow conventional lenders in "treating loans in older urban areas cautiously—resulting in charges of redlining."[51] A congressional study in 1965, for example, argued that only a small fraction of FHA-insured mortgages were for existing homes in blighted central city areas.[52]

In late 1965, FHA Commissioner Phillip Brownstein responded to these criticisms by issuing directives to FHA regional offices.[53] These directives urged that FHA activities in older inner cities not be confined to urban renewal areas and that Section 221(d)(2) mortgage insurance be used in nondeclared urban renewal areas and even in "neighborhoods in which blighting influences have started decay." These directives helped define the notion of acceptable risk underlying Section 221(d)(2) insurance. However, the economic soundness criterion was still used to evaluate mortgage insurance provided under Section 203(b).

In 1966, Section 203(b) insurance was modified by Section 302 of the Demonstration Cities and Metropolitan Development Act, which added Section 203(1) to the National Housing Act of 1934. This new section applied the acceptable risk criterion to Section 203(b) insurance and specifically noted the need for providing mortgage insurance in inner-city areas, including those experiencing or threatened by riots and disorders. Moreover, in summer 1967, Commissioner Brownstein urged FHA regional offices not to designate entire areas as ineligible for insurance and not to limit FHA activity in the inner city to the Section 221(d)(2) program. FHA approvals in high-risk areas rose from 200 to 1,000 per week during 1967.[54]

Section 103 of the Housing and Urban Development Act of 1968 repealed Section 203(1), replacing it with Section 223(e). This section allowed mortgage insurance to be extended under any FHA program in areas where economic soundness or related considerations would normally preclude eligibility.

The 1968 act designated troubled urban areas as worthy of special consideration, including waiver of statutory limitations concerning loan-to-value ratio, size of unit, or maximum mortgage amount. The aim of Section 223(e) was to provide insurance in "older, declining urban areas" where one or more eligibility requirement for mortgage insurance could not be met, provided that (1) the area was "reasonably viable" and (2) the property was "an acceptable risk." The terms of the mortgages insured under this provision were to be designed with consideration for the needs of "families of low and moderate income in such areas."

It was explicitly recognized that Section 203(b) and Section 221(d)(2) mortgage insurance issued pursuant to Section 223(e) would not be economically sound. Consequently, the 1968 act established a Special Risk Insurance Fund (SRIF) for which appropriations were authorized. This fund was to be used to fulfill insurance obligations under the subsidized programs and certain other mortgage insurance programs, including Section 223(e). As expected, these programs immediately incurred losses.

The effects of Section 223(e) quickly manifested. FHA activity in central cities rose quickly during 1969, with Section 223(e) activity leading the way in declining areas. A dramatic increase in foreclosures and losses followed. In response, the FHA tried to improve the administration of Section 223(e). The resulting administrative changes reduced default losses and the level of FHA activity. In 1976, fewer than 7,500 mortgages, or less than 14% of the program's peak volume in 1969, were insured pursuant to Section 223(e). These efforts notwithstanding, the insurance position of the SRIF—that is, the excess of insurance reserves over estimated reserve requirements— was still –$394 million as of June 30, 1975.

FHA insurance activity became tantamount to a large-scale experiment in inner-city mortgage lending. Units that might never have qualified for private or government-insured financing in the past were approved for FHA mortgage insurance.

Default rates for mortgages insured under Sections 203 and 221 began rising after the passage of Section 223(e) in 1968. These rates peaked in 1972, reaching levels of 2.15% for Section 203(b) mortgages and 6.11% for Section 221 mortgages. Compared to pre-1968 default rates, these figures represent an increase in 203(b) and 221 defaults of roughly 50% for Section 203(b) mortgages and more than 100% for Section 221 loans.

Caution should be exercised in attributing these shifts to Section 223(e). However, the orders of magnitude observed for the 203(b) program are quite consistent with cross-section estimates of relative default probabilities obtained from FHA data. It is also noteworthy that default rates did decline after the administrative reforms implemented in response to the loss experience under 223(e).

These outcomes promoted considerable debate concerning the purpose of legislation that encouraged, if not forced, the FHA to expand its activities in the inner city. Was the mandate simply to stop large-scale redlining (refusal to lend in certain sections of cities)? Alternatively, was the mandate to assume the burden of providing high-risk credit in the hope of saving inner-city neighborhoods?

Whatever the intent, expansion of FHA insurance in the inner city can be viewed as an experiment in determining the influence of neighborhood characteristics on default. The pattern of making loans through federal insurance programs that private lenders viewed as "too risky" bears a superficial resemblance to the pattern observed in the initial Section 203(b) program during the 1930s. However, the two historical episodes have at least two major differences.

First, expanded FHA activity in risky neighborhoods resulted in the approval of many economically unsound mortgages. As discussed in the next section, some community groups said FHA-insured mortgages accelerated neighborhood decline by undermining incentives for property maintenance.[55] Private lenders did not likely view this as an experiment worthy of emulation.

Second, even if lenders wanted to follow the FHA example, neighborhood characteristics are more difficult to quantify than loan terms, which are easily reduced to a loan-to-value ratio or mortgage term. As a result, it is more difficult to translate neighborhood characteristics into measures of risk.

Government Regulation of Conventional Mortgage Lenders

The expansion of FHA mortgage insurance and housing subsidies during the 1960s and 1970s was perceived as less than completely successful in achieving the social objectives intended. Several explanations were offered. Racial discrimination was cited as one barrier to the efficient and equitable functioning of urban housing markets.

Paradoxically, the increase in FHA activity during the 1960s and 1970s was criticized as contributing to urban housing problems. This opinion is reflected in the following statement in a report by the Congressional Budget Office:[56]

> *Prospective buyers or repairers of homes in redlined areas either are unable to finance their desired actions or must use FHA, VA, and Farmers' Home insured or guaranteed financing.*

Unfortunately, federally underwritten mortgages in central city areas have been subject to abuse, often resulting in overpayment for poor quality housing and later abandonment. Lack of conventional financing thus produces substantial losses for potential buyers and sellers in affected areas and for their neighbors as neighborhood decline is hastened.

Concern about discrimination in housing markets was manifested in the Fair Housing Act (Title VIII) in 1968 and the Equal Credit Opportunity Act in 1974. Both regulations defined criteria that lenders may and may not use in their lending decisions.[57] In general, both acts prohibited lenders from denying or limiting credit solely on the basis of race, sex, creed, or national origin. In addition, the Fair Housing Act permitted lenders to take some neighborhood characteristics into account, but not others. Characteristics that are permissible include

- The condition or design of the property, or of nearby properties that clearly affect the value of that property
- The availability of neighborhood amenities or city services
- The need of the bank to hold a balanced real estate portfolio, with a reasonable distribution of loans in various neighborhoods, types of property, and loan amounts

However, lenders are enjoined from

- Denying or restricting mortgage credit in certain neighborhoods in the lender's service area because of race, color, religion, or national origin of the residents
- Relying on appraisals that assign a lower value to a neighborhood because of a mix of races and national origins
- Equating a racially mixed neighborhood with a deteriorating neighborhood
- Incorporating the idea that deterioration of a neighborhood is inevitable
- Equating age of the property with the value of the property
- Prescreening loan applicants

The Home Mortgage Disclosure Act of 1975 and the Community Reinvestment Act of 1977 are aimed at increasing the volume of conventional loans in redlined areas. The HMDA requires lenders to disclose the location of their loans, though, interestingly enough, not deposits. The CRA represents an increased effort to prod lenders to expand mortgage lending in older and moderate-income areas in which they have offices.

Lenders deemed in violation of the Fair Housing Act are assumed, *a priori,* to violate performance standards of the Community Reinvestment Act. Consequently, the forms of lender behavior described previously are also proscribed under the CRA. However, the range of lender behavior subject to scrutiny is wider under the CRA than under the Fair Housing Act.

In particular, the CRA places emphasis on possible "errors of omission" that discourage potential borrowers from applying for loans. The Fair Housing Act singles out errors of commission in the form of prescreening. Prescreening is also viewed with suspicion under the Community Reinvestment Act. However, lenders are also judged on whether they make affirmative efforts to encourage applications for credit.

Specific assessment factors are the institution's steps to evaluate the credit needs of its community, including efforts to communicate with the community regarding credit services provided by the institution; and the institution's record of opening and closing offices and providing services at offices.

By implication, lenders that devote more resources to identifying community needs in some neighborhoods than in others, or that open (or close) offices in some neighborhoods but not in others, could violate the standards of the Community Reinvestment Act.

Summary

For millions of households around the globe, housing is one of the most important assets. Homeownership rates differ not only over time in individual countries, but also across countries at the same point in time. The tendency has been for homeownership to increase with urbanization and economic development. Important public- and private-sector innovations in home finance include the growth of specialized institutions, mortgage insurance, securitization of mortgages, and use of covered bonds. These types of innovation play different roles in different countries, with the result that mortgage debt–to–GDP ratios vary substantially. No single strategy will address all the world's housing needs.

Endnotes

1 This chapter draws heavily on earlier articles co-authored by James R. Barth.

2 Michael R. Haines and Allen C. Goodman, "A Home of One's Own: Aging and Homeownership in the United States in the Late Nineteenth and Early Twentieth Centuries," NBER Working Paper, no. 21 (January 1991).

3 See *The Economist*, "Bricks and Slaughter: A Special Report on Property," March 5, 2011.

4 See Michael Lea, "International Comparison of Mortgage Product Offerings." Special Report, Research Institute for Housing America, Mortgage Banker Association, September 2010.

5 Lynn M. Fisher and Austin J. Jaffe, "Determinants of International Homeownership Rates," Housing Finance International, September 2003.

6 Ashok Bardhan and Robert H. Edelstein, "Housing Finance in Emerging Economies: Applying a Benchmark from Developed Countries," in ed. Danny Shahar, Seow Eng Ong, and Charles Leung, *Mortgage Markets Worldwide* (Oxford, U.K.: Blackwell Publishing Ltd., 2009). Also see Michael Lea, "Alternative Forms of Mortgage Finance: What Can We Learn From Other Countries?" paper prepared for Harvard Joint Center for Housing Studies National Symposium, *Moving Forward: The Future of Consumer Credit and Mortgage Finance*, Harvard Business School, 18 February 2010.

7 See Richard K. Green and Susan M. Wachter, "The American Mortgage in Historical and International Context," *Journal of Economic Perspectives* 19, no. 4 (2005): 93–114.

8 Section 3 is drawn heavily from James R. Barth and Martin Regalia, "The Evolving Role of Regulation in the Savings and Loan Industry," in ed. Catherine England and Thomas F. Huertas, *The Financial Services Revolution: Policy Directions for the Future* (Boston: Kluwer Academic Press, 1988).

9 The Housing and Urban Development Act of 1968 authorized federal savings and loan associations to offer savers deposit accounts rather than share accounts. The Federal Home Loan Bank Board adopted a regulation implementing this legislation, and all federal associations began offering deposit accounts the following year.

10 The first savings and loan associations were essentially finite-lived mutual funds, investing shareholders' savings solely in residential mortgage loans. There were no maturity mismatch problems, and informational problems were minimized by direct saver involvement in every aspect of the business.

11 Credit unions did not come into existence until the early 1900s.

12 James R. Barth and M.A. Regalia (1988).

13 See Bodfish, Morton. *History of Building and Loans in the United States,* Chicago: U.S. Building and Loan League, 1931.

14 See Bodfish (1931) and Bodfish (1935). *Note:* Apparently, the state governments initially became involved as a cost-effective means for most associations to impose some discipline on all associations, to maintain the reputation of every association.

15 In 1875, New York was the first state to pass legislation requiring the filing of annual reports.

16 See Bodfish (1931).

17 *Ibid.*

18 See Bodfish and Theobald (1940).

19 D.M. Frederiksen, "Mortgage Banking in America," *Journal of Political Economy* 2, no. 2 (March 1984): 203–234.

20 See Bodfish (1931).

21 According to Bodfish (1935), "One-half of the counties in the United States as a result of the Great Depression now had no mortgage loan institutions or facilities."

22 The institutions initially eligible for membership were savings and loan associations, insurance companies, and mutual savings banks. The latter two types of institutions generally did not join the system.

23 See Bodfish and Theobald (1940).

24 See Bodfish (1935).

25 The federal government, for example, introduced the Home Affordable Modification Program in March 2009 to encourage lenders and services to modify the terms of the mortgage contract in a way that increases affordability for homeowners. The government introduced the Emergency Homeowner's Loan Program in August 2010 to provide interest-free loans to borrowers to pay arrearages plus a portion of their monthly mortgage when the borrowers experienced a significant loss of income. (See James Orr, John Sporn, Joseph Tracy, and Junfeng Huang, "Help for Unemployed Borrowers: Lessons from the Pennsylvania Homeowners' Emergency Mortgage Assistance Program," *Current Issues in Economics and Finance* 17, no. 2 (2011).

26 The act specified that most loans had to be mortgage loans and had to be secured by houses within 50 miles of the association's home office.

27 In 1975, 83% of all savings and loan associations used the taxable income method. In 1982, the corresponding figure was 65%.

28 Before March 1981, however, FHLBB policy prohibited interstate branching by federally chartered savings and loan associations. Since then, the policy has been modified to permit federal associations to branch on equal terms with state associations and to branch more freely as a result of the acquisition of supervisory or failing institutions. In 1994, the Riegle-Neal Interstate Banking and Branching Efficiency Act allowed for nationwide banking of depository institutions through acquisitions and mergers. Then in 2010, the Dodd-Frank Act allowed all depository institutions to engage in nationwide branching.

29 Indeed, savings and loan associations are now permitted to accept demand deposits insured by the FDIC and make

commercial loans, which is a function that, according to the Bank Holding Company Act, legally defines a bank.

30 This section is drawn heavily from James R. Barth, Joseph Cordes, and Anthony Yezer, "Federal Government Attempts to Influence the Allocation of Mortgage Credit: FHA Mortgage Insurance and Government Regulations," *The Economics of Federal Credit Activity*, U.S. Congressional Budget Office, Washington, DC, October 1980.

31 According to O. Emre Ergungor, "Homeowner Subsidies," *Economic Commentary*, Federal Reserve Bank of Cleveland, February 23, 2011, the fiscal year 2010 budget indicates that "the U.S. government will spend $780 billion in tax expenditures over the next five years to subsidize housing through mortgage interest and property tax deduction."

32 Alex Pollock, Testimony to Subcommittee on Security and International Trade and Finance: Committee on Banking, Housing, and Urban Affairs, United States Senate, September 29, 2010.

33 This section is drawn heavily from James R. Barth, Joseph Cordes and Anthony Yezer (1980).

34 Thomas N. Hertzog, *History of Mortgage Finance with an Emphasis on Mortgage Insurance*, American Society of Actuaries, 2009.

35 See Leo Grebler, David M. Blank, and Louis Winnick, *Capital Formation in Residential Real Estate* (Princeton, N.J.: University Press, 1956), Table 55.

36 Board of Governors of the Federal Reserve System, *Banking Studies* (Baltimore, Md.: Waverly Press, 1977).

37 U.S. Department of Housing and Urban Development, *Future Role of FHA*, 1977.

38 *Ibid.*

39 Leo Grebler, "The Role of Federal Credit Aids in Residential Construction," Occasional Paper 39, National Bureau of Economic Research, 1953.

40 These mortgage limits, which apply nationwide, will also have regional effects due to different rates of growth in housing prices. One might therefore expect more conventional mortgage loans to be made in the East than in the West. This is consistent with the evidence.

41 The modern PMI industry was born in the 1950s but traces its origins to the late 1800s and the founding of title insurance companies in New York. That state passed the first legislation authorizing the insuring of mortgages in 1904 and then, in 1911, allowed title insurance companies to buy and resell mortgages—comparable to today's secondary mortgage market. To make mortgages more marketable, companies offered guarantees of payment as well as title, thus establishing the business of mortgage insurance (see *2009–10 Fact Book,* Mortgage Insurance Companies of America).

42 According to Dwight Jaffee, "Monoline Restrictions, with Applications to Mortgage Insurance and Title Insurance," *Review of Industrial Organization* 28 (2006): 83–108, there were conflicts of interest within the mortgage insurance industry. He points out that the "largest conflict was that the mortgage insurers were also acquiring mortgages, then reselling them within insured pools (an early form of mortgage securitization). As mortgage default rates rose, the insurers fraudulently placed bad loans in insured pools."

43 *Ibid.* Jaffee points out that the coverage amount is typically the first 20%–30% of the lost mortgage principal. He also notes that, in Australia, the standard policy covers 100% of the loan amount. Also see Thomas N. Herzog, "History of Mortgage Finance With an Emphasis on Mortgage Insurance," Society of Actuaries, 2009.

44 It should be noted that, under temporary authority granted in 1974, the Government National Mortgage Association, which was chartered by federal law in its present form in 1968, also purchased conventional insured mortgages. However, GNMA's general purchase authority is restricted to the purchase of mortgages insured or guaranteed by the federal government.

45 *Ibid.*

46 See Congressional Budget Office, "An Overview of Federal Support for Housing," Economic and Budget Issue Brief, November 3, 2009.

47 Leo Grebler, *The Role of Federal Credit Aids in Residential Construction* (NBER, 1953).

48 This section is drawn heavily from James R. Barth, Joseph Cordes, and Anthony Yezer (1980); and James R. Barth with Tong Li, Wenling Lu, Tripon Phumiwasana, and Glenn Yago, *The Rise and Fall of the U.S. Mortgage and Credit Markets: A Comprehensive Analysis of the Meltdown* (Hoboken, New Jersey: John Wiley & Sons, 2009).

49 It should be noted that, under temporary authority granted in 1974, the Government National Mortgage Association, which was chartered by federal law in its present form in 1968, also bought conventional insured mortgages. However, GNMA's general authority is restricted to the purchase of mortgages insured or guaranteed by the federal government.

50 This section is drawn heavily from James R. Barth, Joseph Cordes, and Anthony Yezer (1980).

51 Department of Housing and Urban Development, "Future Role of FHA," 1977.

52 Defaults on FHA-Insured Home Mortgages, Detroit, Michigan, H. Rept. 1152, 92:2 (1965): 51.

53 "Real Estate Settlement Costs, FHA Mortgage, Foreclosures, Housing Abandonment, and Site Selection Policies," House Committee on Banking and Currency, 1965.

54 Peter M. Greenstone, C. Duncan MacRae, and Carla I. Petrone, The Effects of FHA Activity in Older, Urban, Declining Areas; A Review of Existing, Related Analysis, Research Report," (Washington, DC: The Urban Institute, February 1975).

55 For a discussion of this issue, see Kenneth F. Phillips and Michael B. Teitz, "Housing Conservation in Older Urban Areas; A Mortgage Insurance Approach" Berkeley Institute of Governmental Studies, University of California, 1978.

56 Congressional Budget Office, Housing Finance; Federal Programs and Issues, September 23, 1976.

57 For detailed discussion of the problem of identifying and detecting redlining, see James R. Barth, Joseph J. Cordes, and Anthony M.J. Yezer (1980).

3

Turmoil in Global Housing Markets: Implications for the Future of Housing Finance

In the wake of the global financial crisis of 2007–2009, it is important to understand the implications of this economic tsunami for the future of housing finance, not just in the United States, but around the world. We begin with the collapse of the housing and mortgage markets in the U.S.

The U.S. Housing Crisis[1]

The residential mortgage market in the United States has worked extremely well over the past two centuries, enabling millions to achieve the dream of homeownership. The homeownership rate reached a record high of 69.2% in the second quarter of 2004 before declining to 65.9% at the end of the second quarter in 2011 (see Figure 3.1), with all segments of society participating during the rate-increasing period.

To be sure, these markets have known periods of turmoil. After the Great Depression, the first major episode was the collapse of the savings and loan (S&L) industry in the early 1980s. This led to significant changes in mortgage markets.[2]

Figure 3.1   Homeownership rate reached an all-time high in 2004 (1965–2011).

Source: U.S. Census Bureau.

When the Federal Reserve changed its policy to combat inflationary pressures in the late 1970s, short-term interest rates rose rapidly and the yield curve inverted, with short-term rates exceeding longer-term rates.[3] At the time, savings and loans were heavily involved in the mortgage market, holding about half of all mortgage loans in portfolio. The vast majority of these loans were traditional fixed-rate, 30-year mortgages. The inverted yield curve meant nearly all savings and loans were insolvent if their mortgage portfolios had been marked to market because the interest rates on their outstanding mortgage loans were lower than the rates on Treasury securities of comparable maturity as well as newly issued mortgage loans. The nearly 4,000 savings and loans in existence at the time were estimated to be insolvent on this basis by roughly $150 billion[4] (or $417 billion in 2011 dollars). However, institutions were not required to mark to market their mortgage portfolios.

The reason for this dire situation was that the savings and loan institutions were largely prohibited from offering adjustable-rate mortgages or hedging their interest-rate risk through the use of derivatives. Congress responded to the crisis by broadening the powers of savings and loans so they could operate more like commercial banks, which largely avoided the same plight. Furthermore, savings and loans were also allowed to offer adjustable-rate mortgages.

This financial innovation enabled savings and loans to shift some of the interest-rate risk to borrowers. Although adjustable-rate mortgages accounted for less than 5% of originations in 1980, that share increased to 64% in 2006 before declining to 37% in 2010 as a result of the financial crisis.[5]

The broader powers of savings and loans also meant a blurring of distinctions among different types of depository institutions. The share of home mortgages held by savings institutions dropped from 50% in 1980 to 8% in 2006, to less than 7% in 2010. Commercial banks saw their share rise from 16% to 21% over the same period.

The percentage increase for commercial banks may seem relatively small, but the total assets of commercial banks in 2010 was $12 trillion, compared to the savings institutions' $1 trillion in assets. These figures indicate that commercial banks are now more important for financing housing than saving institutions.

The second episode of disruption emerged in summer 2007, triggered by the "subprime mortgage market meltdown." The 1980s S&L crisis was more regional in nature, while the subprime damage was truly national in scope.

Millions of households with subprime loans (loans made to less creditworthy individuals) became delinquent on their mortgages, and many lost their homes to foreclosure. Many of these homebuyers took out "hybrid" mortgage loans, which featured low introductory interest rates for two or three years but a higher rate thereafter.

This financial innovation was fine as long as home prices continued to rise. With increases in home prices, borrowers could refinance their mortgages at lower interest rates as they built up equity. Such individuals had the opportunity to improve their credit ratings at the same time.

Unfortunately, home prices fell—and fell dramatically. This led to a rise in foreclosures and a tightening of credit standards by lenders that triggered the housing market meltdown and ushered in a more general financial crisis and recession. As of the writing of this book, the pain that began in the housing sector was still being felt throughout the economy. This underscores the importance of promoting well-functioning housing markets in countries around the globe.

Changes in U.S. mortgage markets over the past three decades contributed to the most recent crisis. Before 1980, as already noted, S&Ls made the vast majority of mortgage loans. These institutions originated, serviced, and held these loans in their portfolios. But as early as 1970, the practice of combining these three functions within a single institution began to change, as mortgage loans were increasingly securitized.

In subsequent years, the Government National Mortgage Association (GNMA, or Ginnie Mae), the Federal National Mortgage Association (FNMA, or Fannie Mae), and the Federal Home Loan Mortgage Corporation (FHLMC, or Freddie Mac) became the primary securitizers of home mortgages. These three entities securitized only 1% of all outstanding mortgages in 1965, but their share rose to a high of 48% in 2001 before declining during the financial crisis and then subsequently returning to 48% in 2009 (see Figure 3.2).

Furthermore, financial institutions themselves began to securitize mortgages, referred to as private-label-backed mortgage pools, which was an innovation. Figure 3.2 shows that their share of home mortgages was less than 1% in 1984 but then increased to a high of 21% in 2006 before declining to 14% in 2009. The private-label-backed mortgage pools increased significantly before the financial crisis and then declined abruptly during and after the crisis. As of mid-2011, nearly all securitization of mortgages was being done by Ginnie Mae, Fannie Mae, and Freddie Mac. The role of private-label securitizers in financing housing had become virtually nonexistent.

Securitization, including that by the private-label firms, contributed to the unbundling of the home mortgage process. Depository institutions no longer had to hold these mortgages in their portfolios. At the same time, investors in mortgage-backed securities provided an additional source of funding beyond deposits of financial institutions.

The origination and servicing of mortgages became separate functions not performed entirely by financial institutions. In this regard, there were 7,000 U.S. mortgage brokers in 1987, but that figure increased to 53,000 by 2006 before declining during and after the financial crisis. Their share of mortgage originations increased from 20% in 1987 to 68% in 2003 before declining to 58% in 2006 and even more so thereafter (see Figures 3.3 and 3.4).

Figure 3.2 Securitization significantly reduced the importance of financial institutions in funding home mortgages (1952–2010).

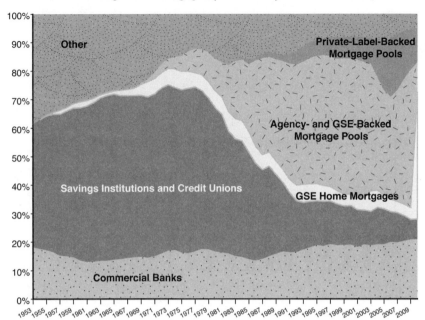

Note: "Other" includes funding from life insurance companies, private pension funds, state and local government employee retirement funds, finance companies, and real estate investment trusts.
Source: Federal Reserve.

The unbundling of the mortgage process into these three separate functions (funding, origination, and servicing) meant there were three sources of revenue to be earned. Unlike the savings and loans, and even the commercial banks, investors who bought securities based on pools of mortgage loans became further removed from the homes serving as collateral; therefore, they relied heavily on rating agencies to accurately assess the credit quality of these securities. For many investors, this proved to be a mistake.

Securitization and adjustable-rate mortgages contributed to the development of the U.S. mortgage markets by providing more diverse sources of funding for home mortgages and a wider choice of mortgage products for consumers. Increased use of adjustable-rate mortgages also allowed lenders and borrowers to share the interest risk.

Figure 3.3   Mortgage brokerages became major players in originating home mortgages (1987–2006).

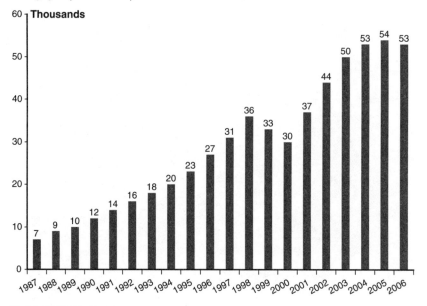

Source: Wholesale Access.

Figure 3.4   Mortgage brokers accounted for the majority of recent mortgage originations (1987–2006).

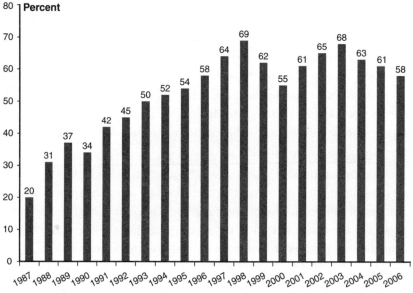

Source: Wholesale Access.

Borrowers who chose adjustable-rate mortgages typically received an initial interest rate that was lower than what they could obtain with a fixed-rate mortgage, but then they faced the prospect of higher rates. At the same time, the development and wide use of credit scores for individual borrowers and credit ratings for individual issuances of mortgage-backed securities provided more information for lenders and borrowers to better assess and price risk—or, at least, that was the goal.

Beginning in the second half of the 1990s, subprime mortgage loans grew rapidly in importance. The subprime share of total originations was less than 5% in 1994, increased to 13% in 2000, and then grew to more than 20% in 2005 and 2006 before declining to 0.3% in 2010 and at the end of second quarter of 2011 (see Figure 3.5). Furthermore, the share of subprime originations packaged into mortgage-backed securities (MBSs) more than doubled over the same period, from 31.6% to 80.5%, before declining to zero in 2010 and at the end of second quarter of 2011 (see Table 3.1).

The subprime mortgage market essentially shut down in 2009 and in the subsequent year and a half. But this was not all that was happening. MBSs were put into pools and new securities were issued, referred to as collateralized debt obligations (CDOs). The issuers of CDOs were the major buyers of the low-rated classes of subprime MBSs in 2006.[6] CDOs were also put into pools and still newer securities, known as "CDOs-squared," were issued.

As already noted, Ginnie Mae, Freddie Mac, and Fannie Mae no longer overwhelmingly dominated security issuance. Home mortgage loans securitized by nonagency entities grew from $386 billion in 2000 to $2.2 trillion in the third quarter of 2007. The growth of subprime lending and nonagency securitization was stimulated by relatively low interest rates and increased reliance on credit scoring and risk-based pricing.

The ten-year Treasury note rate fell from 6% in 2000 to 4% in 2003, rose to 4.8% in 2006, and declined to 3.3% at year-end 2010.

Lending institutions and investors seeking higher yields in the earlier years of the decade found the subprime market attractive but apparently underestimated the risks. At the same time, the prospect of subprime loans coupled with rising home prices undoubtedly enticed borrowers in many parts of the country.

Figure 3.5   Subprime took an increasing share of all home mortgage originations (2001 to first half of 2011).

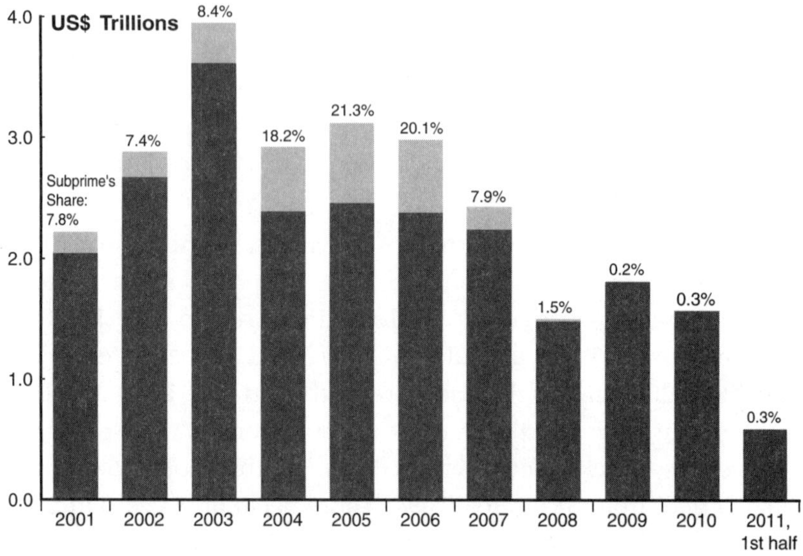

Sources: *Inside Mortgage Finance*, Milken Institute.

Home prices jumped nationally at an average annual rate of nearly 9% from 2000 to 2006 after rising an average of slightly less than 3% per year in the 1990s (see Figure 3.6). Stated another way, a home worth $150,000 in 2000 was worth $251,565 in 2006. This environment undoubtedly fueled optimism on the part of lenders, borrowers, and investors.

Subprime loans also lured mortgage brokers, who could earn fees while passing along any credit risk to others. These brokers were frequently paid fees by lenders for finding customers for home loans.

Although lenders had in-house mortgage brokers, they turned increasingly to outside brokers to accommodate more would-be homebuyers. Obviously, outside operations were harder for the lenders to monitor. At the same time, the prospect of earning more fees gave outside brokers an incentive to qualify as many borrowers as possible. After the financial crisis became full blown, lenders shifted their operations to rely more on their own brokers than outsiders. This led to a substantial decline in the number of independent mortgage brokers.

Table 3.1   Growing Importance of Subprime and Securitization of Home Mortgage Originations (1994 to first half of 2011)

Year	Total Originations (US$ Billions)	Prime Market Share of Total (%)	Subprime Market Share of Total (%)	Subprime MBS Market Share of Total (%)	Share of Subprime MBS of Subprime Originations (%)
1994	773	94.0	4.5	1.4	31.6
1995	639	86.9	10.2	2.9	28.4
1996	785	83.2	12.3	4.5	36.4
1997	859	78.3	14.5	7.3	50.0
1998	1,450	84.0	10.3	5.7	55.1
1999	1,310	83.2	12.2	4.6	37.9
2000	1,048	81.5	13.2	5.3	40.5
2001	2,215	87.9	7.8	4.3	55.2
2002	2,885	88.4	7.4	4.2	57.1
2003	3,945	86.5	8.4	5.1	61.0
2004	2,920	68.1	18.2	13.7	75.7
2005	3,120	62.4	21.3	16.3	76.3
2006	2,980	63.7	20.1	16.2	80.5
2007	2,430	83.1	7.9	9.0	114.8
2008	1,500	98.3	1.5	0.2	9.8
2009	1,815	99.8	0.2	0.0	21.8
2010	1,570	99.7	0.3	0.0	0.0
2011 (first half)	590	99.7	0.3	0.0	0.0

Source: The 2011 Mortgage Market Statistical Annual, *Inside Mortgage Finance.*

In summer 2007, several subprime lenders filed for bankruptcy, and other financial firms suffered heavy losses on subprime securities. The storm clouds had been gathering for years.

The rate of foreclosures on subprime loans increased—by some estimates, nearly doubling—from 2000 to 2006. For loans made in 2006, the foreclosure rate was 5.5% after just six months from origination. This exceeded the corresponding rates for all previous years.

Figure 3.6   Home prices peaked in 2006 and subsequently declined.
(1st Quarter 1991–2nd Quarter 2011; Index, 1st Quarter 1991=100)

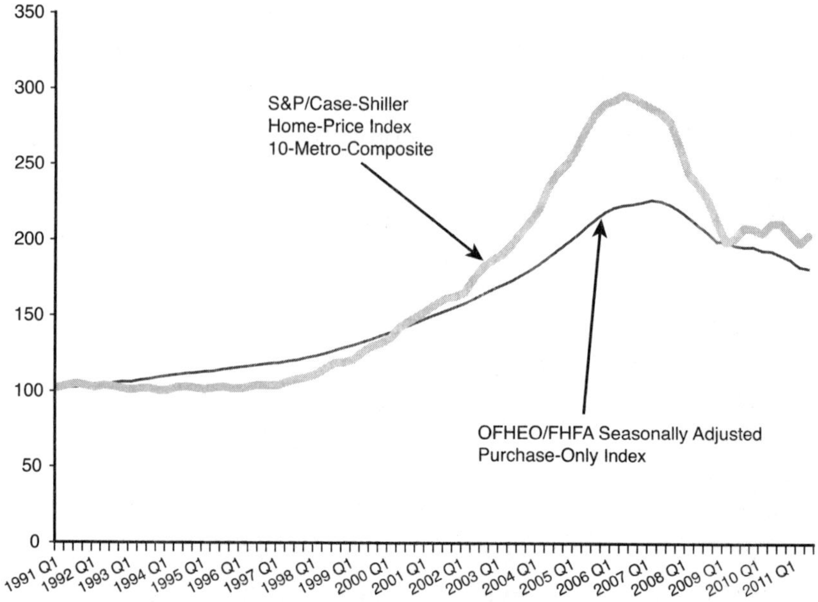

Source: S&P/Case-Shiller (Bloomberg) and OFHEO/FHFA.

Most subprime foreclosures occurred in the first few years after the loans were made. Based on LoanPerformance data, the national foreclosure rate on subprime mortgages originated in 2006 was slightly higher than 10% from January 2006 through September 2007, and nearly 20% for loans made in California. As of November 2007, there was one foreclosure for every 617 households, according to RealtyTrac.

This led to many condemnations of subprime mortgages, particularly hybrid loans or loans with interest rate resets. The process of securitizing loans was questioned. Some critics argued that subprime borrowers should not have been offered many of the innovative financial products that became available before the housing market collapse.

It is important to remember, however, that the growth in this market reflected a combination of factors, including the increase in first-time homeownership attributable to less rigorous screening of loan seekers. Subprime loans also let some borrowers improve their credit scores and then qualify as prime borrowers.

The distinction between prime and subprime borrowers is not as clear-cut as one might think, as Figure 3.7 illustrates. The data from LoanPerformance show that prime borrowers can have FICO scores below 400, while subprime borrowers can score above 820. There is no standard industry-wide definition of the term *subprime*. This means each lender makes its own determination.[7] In fact, if appropriate risk-based pricing is used, the distinction between prime and subprime lending becomes artificial.

Figure 3.7   Distribution of prime and subprime mortgage originations by FICO score (2006).

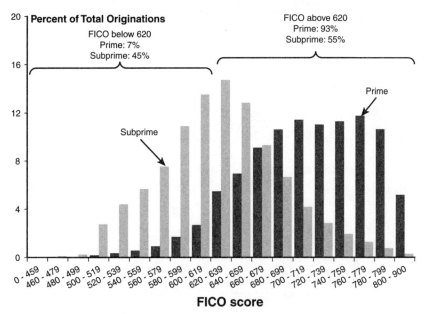

Source: LoanPerformance.

Furthermore, as Figures 3.8 and 3.9 show, most of the same types of mortgage products offered to subprime borrowers were also offered to prime borrowers. And the securitization of these products was important in enhancing the liquidity of mortgage loans and increasing the supply of funds for such loans.

Figure 3.8   Prime mortgage originations (January 1999 to July 2007).

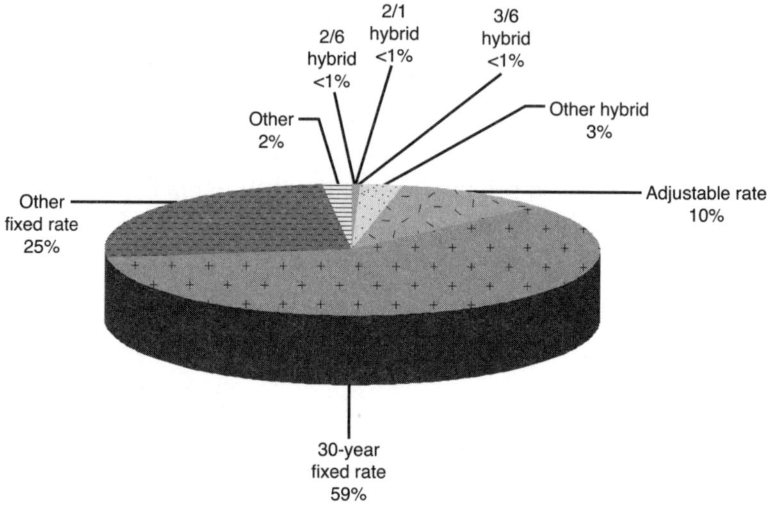

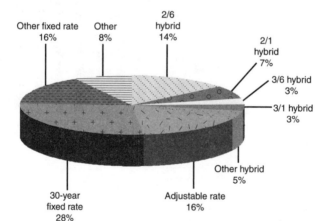

Sources: LoanPerformance, Milken Institute.

Figure 3.9   Subprime mortgage originations (January 1999 to July 2007).

Sources: LoanPerformance, Milken Institute.

Most importantly, the factors that cause individuals to enter foreclosure are generally based not on simply the type of product they receive, but rather on the financial straits they find themselves in after they obtain mortgage loans. These difficulties include unemployment, divorce, health problems, and, especially, a decline in housing prices that leaves homes worth less than their outstanding mortgage balances.

By recognizing the key role these factors play, it becomes clear that additional legislation and regulations cannot—and should not—try to prevent subprime lending (or innovation in the mortgage markets more generally), because that will simply shut off credit to less creditworthy individuals who want to become homeowners.

Instead, efforts should focus on better educating consumers about complex loan products and simplifying the documents necessary for informed decision making. Consumers must be allowed to choose mortgage products, even if some expose borrowers to interest-rate risk.

Also, investors, domestic and foreign, in securities backed by subprime loans—particularly in the more exotic types—must more fully appreciate the fact that the marketplace is sometimes quite harsh in punishing those who seek ever higher returns without taking into account the correspondingly greater risk.

Lastly, in view of the fundamental determinants of foreclosures, more thought should be given to what foreclosure rate is acceptable on subprime mortgage loans. Surely, it would be unreasonable to implement regulations based on the premise that the socially desirable foreclosure rate is zero. If that were the case, hardly anyone would qualify for a mortgage.

Just as it is difficult to distinguish between prime and subprime borrowers on the basis of FICO scores, it is also difficult to distinguish between them on the basis of the mortgage products they use. Over the past decade, most—if not all—of the products offered to subprime borrowers have also been offered to prime borrowers. In fact, from January 1999 through July 2007, prime borrowers obtained 31 of the 32 types of mortgage products—fixed-rate, adjustable-rate, and hybrid mortgages, including those with balloon payments—obtained by subprime borrowers.

Although differences exist in the *extent* to which the same types of mortgage product are offered to prime and subprime borrowers, both groups have had access to a wide range of products. Furthermore, regulators have noted that "subprime lending is not synonymous with predatory lending."[8]

If the loan product itself were the problem in the subprime market, one might expect all borrowers using that product to be facing foreclosure. But this is not the case. Foreclosure rates were rising, as already noted, but the rates differ widely by type of product and borrower. Most important, the foreclosure rates on all mortgage products still fell far short of 100%, which means many borrowers were benefiting from them.

To argue that the product is the source of the problem is to ignore a fundamental truth: The ability or willingness to repay loans depends on financial factors. The marketplace and a borrower's financial circumstances may deteriorate, leading to serious problems, including foreclosure. In some parts of the country, for example, real estate prices fell so far that houses were worth less than the balances owed on them.

In addition, borrowers lost jobs, suffered divorce or serious illness, or otherwise faced severe financial straits. These factors, more than anything else, contributed to increases in foreclosures, regardless of the mortgage product.

Some products, however, did become associated with relatively high and rising foreclosure rates, especially among subprime borrowers. But both prime and subprime borrowers experienced foreclosures for 29 of the mortgage products, indicating that virtually every mortgage product—whether prime or subprime—is a candidate for foreclosure.

Of course, foreclosure rates on subprime mortgages are typically higher than those for prime mortgages, regardless of product type. Subprime borrowers are, by definition, riskier.

Furthermore, as Figure 3.10 shows, the loan-to-value ratio may be a more important determinant mortgage loan risk than the borrower's FICO score. In particular, subprime borrowers received a larger proportion of loans with loan-to-value ratios greater than 80%, as compared to prime borrowers.

So what can we conclude? Product innovation is beneficial, and attempts to curtail such innovation in the mortgage market could deny credit for borrowers who would not otherwise qualify for loans. Legislative or regulatory actions that are too sweeping and severe could limit the availability of mortgage products, denying borrowers a wider menu from which to choose the product that best suits their needs.

Figure 3.10   Mortgage originations: loan-to-value (LTV) ratio (2006).

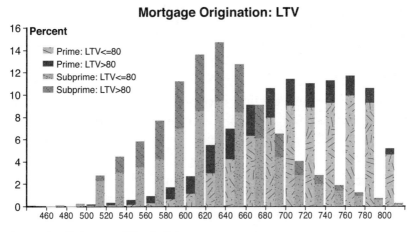

Sources: LoanPerformance, Milken Institute.

Of course, innovative new products require education on the part of lenders and borrowers. If problems arise for lenders, they will make adjustments in the products they offer. Borrowers, too, must educate themselves on which products are most suitable for their current and expected financial status.

The process by which lenders and borrowers decide on specific mortgage products is imperfect and can create difficulties for both at times, resulting in renegotiations of mortgage terms and even the curtailment or discontinuation of some products, as was seen in the recent mortgage market turmoil. Regulatory authorities also should be vigilant against fraudulent activity.

Rising foreclosure rates are a serious issue. But as Lawrence Summers of Harvard University stated in September 2007, "[W]e need to ask ourselves the question, and I don't think the question has been put in a direct way and people have developed an answer; what is the optimal rate of foreclosures? How much are we prepared to accept?"[9]

The same type of argument applies to securitization. Securitization, per se, is not a problem; the quality of the products that are securitized and the creditworthiness of the borrowers present potential problems. For example, to the extent that subprime loans created problems, securities backed by such loans would face similar problems.

Many subprime mortgages were hybrid loans or loans with interest rate resets, as noted earlier. Some of the mayhem in the mortgage market was blamed on interest rates that reset upward after an initial two- or three-year period.

These loans are known as "hybrids" because their interest rates are fixed for a period and then become variable, often with caps that limit the increase over a year or over the term of the loan. A relatively large number of borrowers with shaky credit histories took out hybrid mortgages.

Hybrids typically do not pose problems, as long as home prices rise and individuals refinance their loans before the interest rates reset to a higher level. But as already noted, home prices did not continue rising, and borrowers had trouble refinancing. As a result, foreclosures became more common in recent years.

Because hybrid loans—especially subprime hybrids—have become so controversial, it is important to assess their longer-term role in home foreclosures against other products in the mortgage market. Figure 3.11 shows that subprime borrowers did account for a larger proportion of adjustable rate mortgages than prime borrowers. In addition, Figure 3.12 shows that subprime borrowers received the largest share of hybrid mortgages; Alt-A borrowers, those with little or no documentation of their income or net worth, received the second-largest share of such mortgages; and prime borrowers received the smallest share.

Figures 3.13–3.16 show mortgage originations and cumulative foreclosures for prime and subprime borrowers. The numbers, covering the period from January 1999 to July 2007, before the financial crisis fully emerged, are based on a sample of 80 million mortgage loans from LoanPerformance. Figure 3.13 shows that, of

71 million prime mortgage originations, nearly 84% were fixed-rate mortgages (mostly 30-year, fixed-rate loans), 10% were adjustable-rate mortgages, and fewer than 5% were hybrid mortgages. In contrast, Figure 3.15 shows that, of the 9.5 million subprime mortgage loan originations, 44% were fixed-rate mortgages, 16% were adjustable-rate mortgages, and 32% were hybrid mortgages.

Figure 3.11 The largest share of ARMs went to subprime borrowers (quarterly, 2001 to Q2 2008).

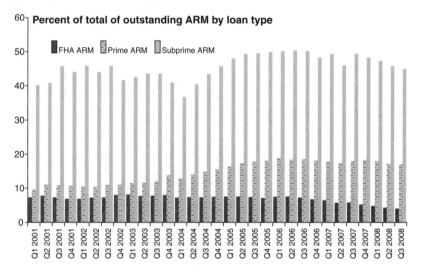

Sources: Mortgage Bankers Association, Milken Institute.

Prime and subprime borrowers used all three loan products, but subprime borrowers relied more heavily on hybrid loans. Most of those were 2/28 and 3/27 mortgages, with short-term, fixed interest rates (two and three years, respectively), followed by variable interest rates for the remaining 28 or 27 years. (The 2/28 mortgages also include 2/6 and 2/1 mortgages, or mortgages that reset after six months and one year, respectively, after the two-year fixed-rate period ends; 3/27 mortgages include 3/6 and 3/1 mortgages, or mortgages that reset after six months and one year after the three-year fixed-rate period ends.)

Figure 3.12 Hybrids dominated subprime home mortgage originations (2006).

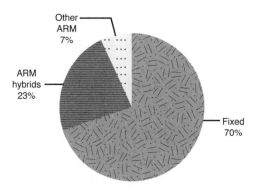

Prime Conventional

Other ARM 7%

ARM hybrids 23%

Fixed 70%

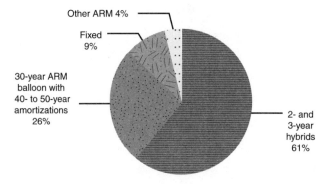

Subprime

Other ARM 4%

Fixed 9%

30-year ARM balloon with 40- to 50-year amortizations 26%

2- and 3-year hybrids 61%

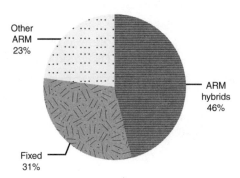

Alt-A

Other ARM 23%

ARM hybrids 46%

Fixed 31%

Source: Freddie Mac.

Figure 3.13 Prime mortgage originations January 1999–July 2007 (Total Number = 70.8 million).

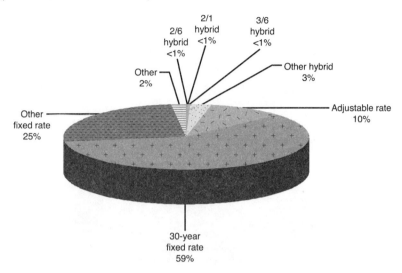

Source: LoanPerformance.

Figures 3.14–3.16 present the cumulative foreclosure starts (and not all starts end in foreclosure) of the different mortgage products. Even though almost all the attention is focused on high and rising foreclosure rates in the subprime market, the total number of foreclosures on *prime* mortgages was slightly higher than the total number of foreclosures on subprime mortgages: 1.4 million versus 1.3 million over the period indicated.

Of all prime mortgage foreclosures, 74% occurred with 30-year, fixed-rate loans. Hybrids and adjustable-rate mortgages accounted for fewer than 12% of foreclosures. In contrast, hybrid loans accounted for 36% of all subprime foreclosures (with 2/28 and 3/27 loans accounting for most of these). Yet fixed-rate loans accounted for nearly as many foreclosures, at 31%, and adjustable-rate loan foreclosures were not far behind, at 26%.

Clearly, a difference exists in the types of products associated with foreclosures for prime and subprime borrowers. It is important to note, however, that more than 800,000 homes financed by subprime loans *other* than hybrid loans went into foreclosure by the end of September 2007, according to data from LoanPerformance. Subprime mortgage foreclosures were obviously a problem, even without taking into account hybrid loans and their interest rate resets.

Figure 3.14   Cumulative foreclosures through September 2007 on prime mortgages originated January 1999–July 2007 (Total Number = 1.4 million).

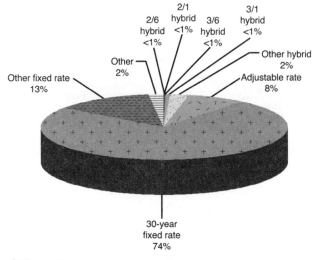

Source: LoanPerformance.

Figure 3.15   Subprime mortgage originations January 1999–July 2007 (Total Number = 9.5 million).

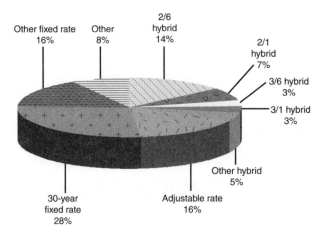

Source: LoanPerformance.

Figure 3.16 Cumulative foreclosures through September 2007 on subprime mortgages originated January 1999–July 2007 (Total Number = 1.3 million).

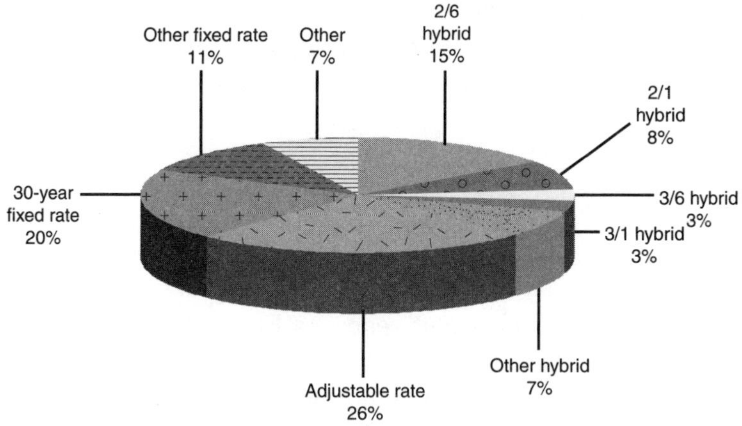

Source: LoanPerformance.

When home prices declined as the financial crisis unfolded, hybrid loans exacerbated the foreclosure problem as more interest rates reset upward, but they were not the basic cause of it. Indeed, all the 2/28 and 3/27 subprime loans in foreclosure as of July 2007—57% and 83%, respectively—had not yet undergone any upward reset of the interest rate.

In the first part of this decade, foreclosures were mainly a problem of the prime mortgage market. In recent years, they became chiefly a problem in the subprime mortgage market. In response to the worsening problems associated with the subprime loans, lenders dramatically reduced the origination of such products, particularly those with reset features. However, many subprime borrowers benefited from the product diversity that provided access to credit and homeownership. Once again, it is important that any legislative or regulatory action not unduly curtail subprime mortgage loans.

A final note: Many subprime borrowers got financing on extremely generous terms. In many cases, lenders extended credit without requiring a down payment. Borrowers were able to take out loans on the basis of the equity they had built up over time in their homes, especially during the period of rapidly increasing home prices. Of course, when home prices declined, many of these owners found that they owed more on their homes, including the first and second lien mortgages, than their homes were worth. This provided an incentive to stop making payments and allow homes to go into foreclosure. Again, the ability and willingness to repay loans matters, not the method of finance.

Housing Problems in Other Countries

The United States was not the only country to endure problems in its housing sector in recent years. As Figure 3.17 (a-c) shows, a number of countries experienced significant increases in housing prices during the past decade before prices declined in nearly all of the ten countries shown by 2009. The two countries that experienced biggest declines in prices were Ireland (–18.5%) and the United States (–12.4%). Portugal experienced a 0.2% increase in prices in 2009. Italy saw a 2% increase in 2008.

Figure 3.17   House price changes in selected countries.

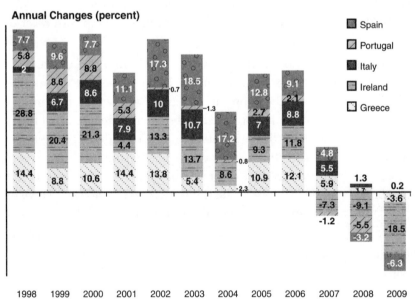

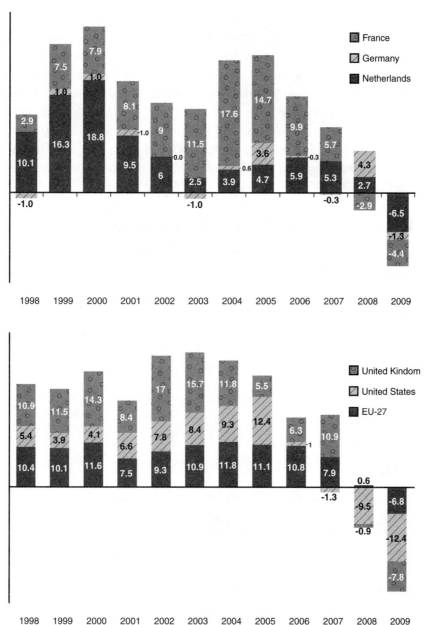

Source: *HYPOSTAT 2009: A Review of Europe's Mortgage and Housing Markets,* November 2010.

From 1998 to 2009, Spain, the United Kingdom, Greece, and Ireland experienced the biggest average increases in home prices and ranked in that order (see Table 3.2). The United States experienced the third-lowest increase in prices, after Germany and Portugal. However, focusing on just the period before the global crisis, Spain had the largest average price increase (12%) from 1998 to 2006, with the United Kingdom, Greece, and Ireland not far behind. The United States ranked eighth, with an average price increase of 6.5%. During the crisis years, Ireland and the United States had the biggest average declines in home prices, at 11.6% and 7.7%, respectively.

Table 3.2   Average House Price Changes in Selected Countries

	1998–2006	**2007–2009**	**1998–2009**
Spain	12.3	–1.6	8.86
United Kingdom	11.3	0.7	8.63
Greece	10.3	1.3	8.06
Ireland	14.6	–11.6	8.06
EU-27	10.4	0.6	7.93
France	9.9	–0.5	7.29
Italy	7.7	3.4	6.85
Netherlands	8.6	0.5	6.60
United States	6.5	–7.7	2.98
Portugal	4.0	–2.2	2.47
Germany	0.6	0.9	0.68

Source: *HYPOSTAT 2009: A Review of Europe's Mortgage and Housing Markets,* November 2010.

Table 3.3 provides information on homeownership rates for the same countries included in Table 3.2. Comparing these two tables illustrates that there is not always a one-to-one correspondence between price increases and homeownership rates. Germany had the lowest homeownership rate among the countries and the lowest average increase in home prices during 1998–2009. It even had the lowest average price increase during the period preceding the global financial crisis. Spain, on the other hand, had the highest homeownership rate and the highest average increase in home prices during both periods. However, other countries, such as Italy, had relatively modest average increases in home prices but relatively high homeownership rates.

Table 3.3 Homeownership Rates (%) for Selected Countries

Country	%
Germany	43
Netherlands	57
France	57
United States	67
EU-27	68
United Kingdom	70
Ireland	75
Portugal	76
Greece	80
Italy	80
Spain	85

Source: Based on the latest available data from *HYPOSTAT 2009: A Review of Europe's Mortgage and Housing Markets,* November 2010.

The question now becomes, despite the fact that some countries experienced bigger increases in home prices than the United States, why did the U.S. housing market suffer far worse than the markets in these other countries?

For one thing, riskier borrowers increasingly were granted a larger share of mortgage loans, and lending standards were far more lenient in the United States. According to Lea (2010), "First subprime lending was rare or non-existent outside of the U.S. The only country with a significant subprime share was the U.K. (a peak of 8 percent of mortgages in 2006). Subprime accounted for 5 percent of mortgages in Canada, less than 2 percent in Australia and negligible proportions elsewhere."

In the United States borrowers with little or no documentation regarding their income or net worth were able to obtain mortgage loans. Interest-only and negative amortization loans were also made available to many borrowers. Lastly, loan-to-value ratios exceeded 100% in some cases. Although some of these practices existed in other countries, they were far less prevalent than in the United States.[10] In Germany, moreover, the maximum loan-to-value ratio was 80%.

You might think that the country with the highest level of mortgage debt relative to GDP would also be the country with the worst-performing mortgage market. Table 3.4 shows that this country would be the Netherlands. However, as Table 3.2 shows, home prices in the Netherlands rose relatively modestly before the crisis and even rose during the crisis period. The fact that prices did not collapse as in the United States spared the Netherlands problems in its housing market.

In addition, although the Netherlands did extend high loan-to-value mortgages to borrowers, they remained a small minority of total mortgages. The tax subsidy extended to borrowers, moreover, was less in the Netherlands than in the United States.[11]

In contrast to the Netherlands, Ireland had a substantial increase in home prices before the crisis and the biggest collapse in home prices during the crisis, as shown in Table 3.2. Table 3.4 also shows that Ireland had the second-largest mortgage level relative to GDP, at 90%. Its housing market also suffered severely in recent years.

Table 3.4   Mortgage Debt-to-GDP Ratios for Selected Countries

Country	%
Italy	22
Greece	34
France	38
Germany	48
EU-27	52
Spain	65
Portugal	68
United States	81
United Kingdom	88
Ireland	90
Netherlands	106

Source: Based on the latest available data from *HYPOSTAT 2009: A Review of Europe's Mortgage and Housing Markets*, November 2010.

Another difference between the housing markets in the United States and in other countries is that only the United States has government-sponsored enterprises such as Freddie Mac and Fannie Mae. These two financial institutions were chartered by the U.S. government and were expected to not only maximize profits for their shareholders, but also provide mortgage credit to make housing finance more affordable to moderate- and low-income households. Unfortunately, this dual mandate led to the insolvency of both of these giant mortgage institutions, and they were placed into conservatorship by the U.S. government. The actions of these institutions worsened the performance of the housing market in the United States.[12]

Still another important difference between the financing of housing in the United States and in other countries is the use of covered bonds instead of securitization. In Denmark, for example, covered bonds are the dominant source of housing finance, as noted in Chapter 2, "Building Blocks of Modern Housing Finance." This form of financing is an alternative to securitization of mortgages, which has been so important in the United States. The advantage of covered bonds is that the bonds remain on the balance sheets of financial institutions and are collateralized with home mortgages that also remain on the balance sheets. Although covered bonds are extremely important in Denmark, they are used in many other European countries, though to a far lesser degree. During the past decade, Denmark was subjected to greater fluctuations in housing prices than the United States, yet Denmark avoided the housing problems the U.S. experienced. Covered bonds may therefore be a good complement, if not a substitute, for securitization.

Housing Problems in the United States Versus Canada

Comparing the performance of the housing markets in Canada and the United States is instructive. As Figure 3.18 shows, these two countries have fairly similar homeownership rates, and both of these rates have tended to trend upward until the global financial crisis. At the same time, home prices in Canada and United States moved fairly close to one another until 2003, when U.S. prices rose faster and then declined more abruptly and further than those in Canada. Home prices in both countries rose from their lows in 2009 and were increasing in 2010 (see Figure 3.19).

Figure 3.18   Homeownership rates in Canada and the United States.

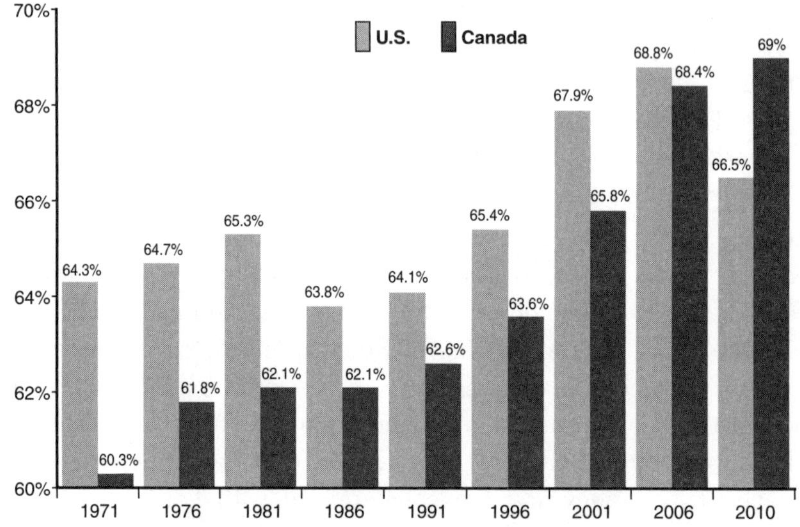

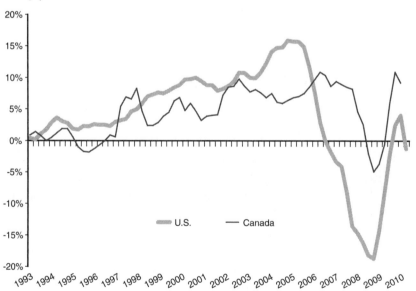

Note: The rate for Canada in 2010 is an estimate from Scotia Economics.

Sources: Statistics Canada, U.S. Census Bureau.

Figure 3.19   Canada and U.S. home prices (year-over-year percentage change).

Sources: S&P Case-Shiller/Fiserv, Bank of Canada, Royal LePage (Q2-2010).

In terms of residential delinquency rates, Figure 3.20 shows that the United States performed far worse than Canada during the global financial crisis. Indeed, the delinquency rate for Canada has remained relatively flat over the entire past decade. This is in sharp contrast to the tremendous rise in the delinquency rate beginning in 2007 in the United States. The question is why the Canadian housing market did not perform in the same troublesome way as the U.S. market, given that both countries have the same general pattern in homeownership rates.

Figure 3.20   Canada and U.S. residential delinquency rates.

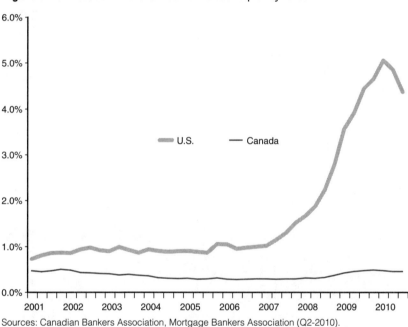

Sources: Canadian Bankers Association, Mortgage Bankers Association (Q2-2010).

One important distinction between Canada and the United States is the extent of government involvement in the housing market. Figures 3.21 and 3.22 show that the U.S. government plays a far greater role in supporting the financing of housing than does the Canadian government.

Financing and mortgage insurance support in the United States is provided by Freddie Mac and Fannie Mae, both of which have specific housing goals set by the U.S. Department of Housing and

Urban Development, and Ginnie Mae.[13] These three institutions provided nearly 60% of the funding for home mortgages in 2006. All three have a mandate to support housing in a way that is not strictly comparable to the approach that would be taken by a firm focusing on risk–return tradeoffs to maximize shareholder value. Canada does have a government-owned mortgage insurance agency, the Canada Housing and Mortgage Corporation, but the insurance provided is not targeted to affordable housing.[14] Canada does not have any entities similar to Freddie Mac and Fannie Mae.

Furthermore, in contrast to the United States, securitization in Canada provided slightly less than 20% of the funding for mortgages in 2006. Banks and credit unions, on the other hand, provided slightly more than 70% of funding in that year.

Canada does not have legislation similar to the Community Reinvestment Act, which was enacted in 1977 to encourage depository institutions to help meet the credit needs of the communities in which they operate, including low- and moderate-income neighborhoods. These differences contributed to greater problems in the housing market in the United States than in Canada.

Figure 3.21   Home mortgage debt outstanding by type of holder for Canada.

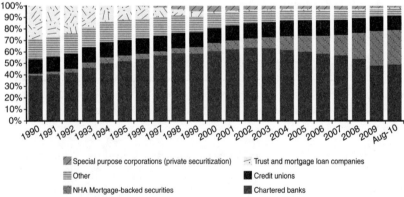

Note: "Other" includes life insurance companies, nondepository credit intermediaries/other financial institutions, and pension funds.

Sources: Canada Mortgage and Housing Corporation, Bank of Canada (through August 2010).

Figure 3.22 Home mortgage debt outstanding, by type of holder, for the United States.

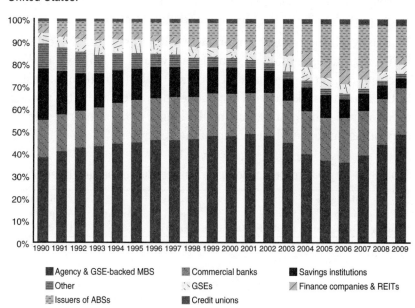

Note: "Other" includes households and nonprofits, nonfarm nonfinancial corporate business, nonfarm noncorporate business, state and local governments (including pension funds), federal government, life insurance companies, and private pensions.

Source: Federal Reserve Flow of Funds (through Q2-2010).

Table 3.5 shows more differences in mortgage finance between Canada and United States. Whereas Americans benefit from a mortgage interest deduction from their taxes, such a benefit is not available to Canadians. In addition, Canadians who become delinquent on their mortgage loans and eventually end up in foreclosure are subject to recourse by lenders. This is not the case in the United States, which provides a greater incentive for individuals to default on their mortgages, especially when they owe more than their homes are worth.

Note further that, in 2006, the subprime share of total outstanding mortgages was less than 5% in Canada, while in the United States, the share was 20%. In addition, Canada relies to a far greater degree on on-balance-sheet funding than the United States, which relies more on securitization. As noted earlier, with a greater degree of subprime mortgages and with a large fraction of them securitized, the result was worse performance of the housing market in United States.

Lastly, Canada relies on mortgages with a fixed rate, typically for five years, but sometimes as short as one year or as long as ten years. The rate is then renegotiated at the end of this period and adjusted to the current market rate. This enables borrowers to better manage their interest-rate risk by changing the length of the fixed-rate period, depending on the level and trend of interest rates.

Table 3.5   Key Differences in Mortgage Finance: Canada versus United States

Country	Mortgage Interest Deduction	Main Product	Recourse	Prepayment penalty	Funding Model	2006 Peak Subprime % Outstanding
Canada	No	5-year FRM	Yes	Yes	On-balance sheet	°Less than 5%
U.S.	Yes	30-year FRM	No	No	Originate-to-distribute	20%

*Subprime mortgages in Canada are mainly near-prime/Alt-A and are much more conservative than in the United States.

Note: FRM refers to fixed-rate mortgages.

Source: Virginie Traclet, "An Overview of the Canadian Housing Finance System," Housing Finance International (Autumn 2010).

Yet another difference between the two countries is that 80% of Canadian homeowners with mortgages had equity that was 20% or more of the value of their homes in 2010. Only 2% of mortgage holders in Canada had negative equity (see Table 3.6). In contrast, about 25% of mortgage holders in United States had negative equity.

Moreover, Canada had more conservative lending policies than the United States during the past decade; the proportion of loans with little or no down payment was far less than in the United States. As Lea (2010) points out, while Canada "relaxed documentation requirements there was far less 'risk layering' or offering limited documentation loans to subprime borrowers with little or no downpayment. There was little 'no doc' lending."[15]

Table 3.6   Positive Equity Is the Norm in Canada

Equity As Percentage of Home Value	Percentage of Mortgage Holders
Negative	2%
0–4.9%	3%
5%–9.9%	6%
10%–19.9%	9%
20% and over	80%

Source: Canadian Association of Accredited Mortgage Professionals (Fall 2010); CoreLogic (*Q2-2010).

Summary

Policymakers must be careful in reacting to the subprime mortgage market turmoil with measures that would curtail credit for those with limited access to traditional mortgage products. A wider range of products is meant to accommodate borrowers with different degrees of risk and to better match risk-and-return combinations. However, it is important to consider factors that caused the U.S. housing market to perform worse than those in other countries, even though its housing price changes were not as extreme.

Endnotes

1 This section draws heavily from James R. Barth, with Tong Li, Wenling Lu, Tripon Phumiwasana, and Glenn Yago, *The Rise and Fall of the U.S. Mortgage and Credit Markets: A Comprehensive Analysis of the Meltdown* (Hoboken, New Jersey: John Wiley & Sons, 2009); and James R. Barth, Tong Li, Triphon Phumiwasana, and Glenn Yago, *Perspectives on Sub-Prime Markets,* Milken Institute Research Report, December 2007.

2 James R. Barth, Susanne Trimbath, and Glenn Yago, eds., *The Savings and Loan Crisis: Lessons from a Regulatory Failure* (Norwell, MA: Kluwer Academic Publishers, 2004).

3 James R. Barth, Tong Li, Triphon Phumiwasana, and Glenn Yago, "Inverted Yield Curves and Financial Institutions: Is the United States Headed for a Repeat of the 1980s Crisis?" *Banks and Banking Systems* 2, no. 3, (2007).

4 James R. Barth, *The Great Savings and Loan Debacle* (Washington, DC: American Enterprise Institute, 1991).

5 Office of Thrift Supervision, *2010 Fact Book: A Statistical Profile of the Thrift Industry* (June 2011).

6 See Richard J. Rosen, "The role of securitization in mortgage lending," Chicago Fed Letter, The Federal Reserve Bank of Chicago, no. 244, November 2007.

7 *Federal Register* (12 July 2002).

8 FDIC press release, "Statement on Subprime Mortgage Lending" (PR-55-2007), 29 June 2007.

9 Lawrence Summers, "Recent Financial Market Disruptions: Implications for the Economy and American Families," panel discussion, The Brookings Institution, Washington, DC, 26 September 2007.

10 See Michael Lea, Testimony to Subcommittee on Security and International Trade and Finance: Committee on Banking, Housing and Urban Affairs, United States Senate, 29 September 2010; and Luci Ellis, "The Housing Meltdown: Why Did It Happen in the United States?" BIS Working Papers, No. 259, Bank for International Settlements, September 2008.

11 See Ellis (2008).

12 James R. Barth, with Tong Li, Wenling Lu, Tripon Phumiwasana, and Glenn Yago, *The Rise and Fall of the U.S. Mortgage and Credit Markets: A Comprehensive Analysis of the Meltdown* (Hoboken, New Jersey: John Wiley & Sons, 2009).

13 *Ibid.*

14 See Michael Lea, Testimony to Subcommittee on Security and International Trade and Finance: Committee on Banking, Housing and Urban Affairs, United States Senate, 29 September 2010.

15 *Ibid.*

4

Housing Finance in the
Emerging Economies

The previous chapters focused mostly on the United States, Europe, and Canada. In this chapter, we turn to the emerging and newly industrializing countries. We start by comparing the depth of mortgage markets in a wide range of countries and then look at the characteristics of housing finance in emerging countries. Finally, we focus in detail on the housing market in China, as it has been totally transformed in the last 30 years or so.

Mortgage Markets in Different Countries

Figure 4.1 shows the depth of mortgage markets in different countries, grouped by region, in terms of the ratio of outstanding mortgages to gross domestic product (GDP), based on the average from 2001 to 2005.[1] On average, the developed countries in Europe, North America, and the Pacific have much greater depth than the emerging markets.

Europe has a great range of ratios. In Italy, the ratio is quite low, at 13.1%. At the other end of the spectrum, the Netherlands has the highest ratio, at 82.7%. The average for the region as a whole is 43.6%. This is about the same as Canada, at 42.9%, and somewhat higher than Japan, at 35.7%. The U.S. is significantly higher, at 67.4%. Most of the other countries fall somewhere in between, except for New Zealand, at 78.2%.

Figure 4.1 The depth of mortgage markets in different countries, by region.

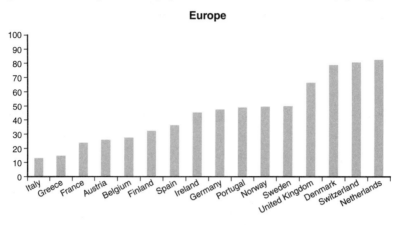

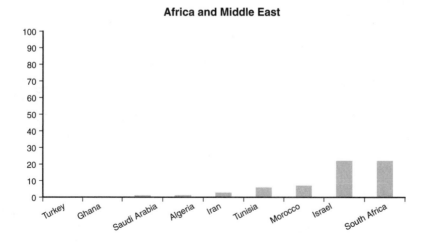

Eastern Europe

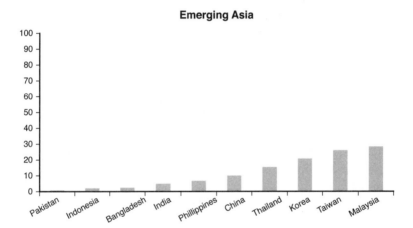

Emerging Asia

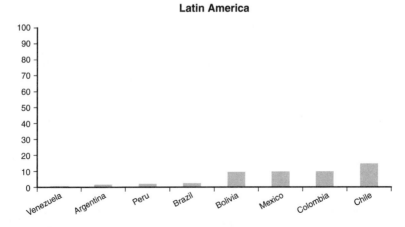

Latin America

Source: V.C. Warnock and F.E. Warnock, "Markets and Housing Finance," *Journal of Housing Economics* (2008): 7.

In contrast, the emerging and newly industrializing countries have much less depth. In Africa and the Middle East, South Africa and Israel have the greatest depth, at 22%. All the other countries are at less than 10%, with most being less than 5%. The story is similar in Eastern Europe, with the maximum being 10.5% in Estonia. In emerging Asia, Malaysia (28.3%), Taiwan (26%), Korea (20.8%), and Thailand (15.5%) all have fairly deep markets. However, the remaining countries do not. China has only 10%.

In Latin America, the highest ratio is in Brazil, at 14.8%, but the rest of the countries' ratios are 10% or less. In short, most emerging and newly industrialized countries do not have much depth in the way of housing finance.

Table 4.1 shows the source of funding for home mortgages in emerging and newly industrialized countries. You can see that, in most countries, the main lenders are banks and specialized housing finance companies. Most of the funding comes from deposits.

For Croatia, Hungary, and Poland, the deposits and mortgages are in foreign exchange. Covered bonds are used to a significant degree in the Czech Republic, Hungary, and Russia, but not much elsewhere. Mortgage-backed securities are used in Mexico and Malaysia, but even there, the amounts are not large. In other countries, their use is negligible.

Perhaps the most striking fact about the mortgage market characteristics in Table 4.2 is the extent of government support. Many countries have upfront subsidies to first-time buyers and subsidies through savings accounts. Low-income households are widely supported. Housing finance funds and loan guarantees are provided by 11 out of 17 of the countries. Slightly fewer countries, 9 out of 17, allow tax deductions of mortgage interest. Only two countries allow capital gains tax deduction. The other interesting item in the table is the high level of permissible loan-to-value ratios in most countries.

Table 4.1   Source of Funding for Home Mortgages in Emerging and Newly Industrialized Economies (2008)

Country	Main Lenders	Deposits ("fx" if Foreign Currency Funding Is Used and Foreign Currency Loans Are Granted)	Covered Bonds/ Residential Loans Ratio (%)	Residential Mortgage Backed Securities/ Residential Loans Ratio (%)	Notes
Brazil	Brazil banks, nondepository mortgage companies, and government housing companies	Largely (through housing finance schemes, directly and indirectly owned by the government)			Two housing finance systems operate alongside each other: the Sistema Financeiro de Habitação and the Sistema de Financiamento Imobiliário. Only less than 50% of property purchases were financed with mortgages. Under SFH regulations, banks are required to direct 65% of savings deposit balances into real estate lending. A government-owned bank has a 75% share of the housing credit market.
Chile	Banks and mortgage administrators of insurance companies	Depends on the product		2.0	With a share of 58.7%, Hipotecarios No Endosables is by far the most important mortgage instrument, as its flexible terms enjoy growing popularity with banks and borrowers. These mortgages are mainly financed with issuances of long-term senior and subordinated corporate bonds.
China	Banks	Largely			The five large commercial banks, all of which are mostly state owned, have the largest share.
Croatia	Banks (95%) and Bausparkassen	Largely (fx), plus parent bank funds			
Czech Republic*	Banks and Bausparkassen (33%)	Largely	50.6		Revenue interest from mortgage covered bond tax is exempt until 2008.

Table 4.1 Source of Funding for Home Mortgages in Emerging and Newly Industrialized Economies (2008) (continued)

Country	Main Lenders	Deposits ("fx" if Foreign Currency Funding Is Used and Foreign Currency Loans Are Granted)	Covered Bonds/ Residential Loans Ratio (%)	Residential Mortgage Backed Securities/ Residential Loans Ratio (%)	Notes
Hungary	Banks (>50%), mortgage banks (38%), and Bausparkassen (5%)	About half (fx)	45.5		Since the crisis, covered bond funding has been restricted to low-LTV loans and reduced incentives for foreign exchange mortgages.
India	Banks and housing finance companies	Deposits and capital markets, refinancing from National Housing Board		<1.0	Financing through the organized sector continues to account for only less than 30% of the total housing investment in India. HDFC Ltd., a special-purpose vehicle of the National Housing Board, issued its first mortgage-backed security in August 2000.
Indonesia	Banks	Mainly			Only a part (according to estimates, 20%–25%) of the total housing demand is financed by the mortgage sector. The state-owned financial institution has the largest share.

Country	Lenders	Funding		Description
Malaysia	Banks and Treasury Housing Loan Division	Some, plus refinancing through Cagamas plus unsecured debt	4.0	The Treasury Housing Loan Division (12%) provides (subsidized) housing loans to government employees only. The Employees' Provident Fund allows early withdrawal for house ownership. Cagamas are government-promoted secondary mortgage liquidity facilities and are involved not in origination, but only in refinancing. Loans sold to Cagamas are not off balance sheet. Malaysia has issued staff housing loan receivables via Cagamas, to further develop the asset-backed securities market.
Mexico	Banks, nondepository SOFOLES, and housing funds (INFONAVIT and FOVISSSTE 51%)	Largely	10.0	INFONAVIT/FOVISSSTE (funds for housing for workers) loans carry an implicit subsidy. The "Esta es tu casa" program offers upfront subsidies for low-income households willing to buy property. The government offers indirect subsidies to the housing market by explicitly guaranteeing obligations of the Sociedad Hipotecaria Federal (SHF), a government housing finance agency. SHF supports the market for residential mortgage-backed securities (RMBS) by offering mortgage insurance and financial guarantees and by ensuring the liquidity of the market, but it does not issue RMBS itself.
Poland	Universal banks (the three largest players at the end of 2008 had a market share of about 35% for new mortgages)	Largely (fx)	1.0	The share of foreign currency mortgage lending declined to 30% in 2010, from 70% in the precrisis period.

Table 4.1 Source of Funding for Home Mortgages in Emerging and Newly Industrialized Economies (2008) (continued)

Country	Main Lenders	Deposits ("fx" if Foreign Currency Funding Is Used and Foreign Currency Loans Are Granted)	Covered Bonds/ Residential Loans Ratio (%)	Residential Mortgage Backed Securities/ Residential Loans Ratio (%)	Notes
Russia	Banks and mortgage banks and cooperatives	Nonbanks mainly deposits; banks' other means of refinancing are through AHML, securitization, mortgage certificates, and debt obligations	18.2	0.1	The central bank estimates that only 10%–15% of the real estate in Russia is bought using bank loans. In 2009, tax rebates increased for purchasing and building residential property; government support is provided through grants and guarantees to the government-owned AHML, a mortgage liquidity facility.
Singapore	Banks and Housing Development Board				The state-owned Housing Development Board has the largest share.
South Africa	Banks and specialized mortgage institutions, including government agencies	Mainly (including wholesale deposits from pension funds and insurance companies)			The National Housing Finance Corporation provides wholesale financing to financial intermediaries and lends directly to low- and medium-income individuals. The Rural Housing Loan Fund lends to intermediary housing lenders, who, in turn, lend to individual low-income earners.

South Korea	Banks (80%), nonbanks, and finance companies			The Korea National Housing Corporation (KNHC) provides low-income public (rental) housing plus for sale, nonbanks offer bullet loans, and foreign bank–sponsored lenders provide higher-LTV and low-interest loans to bypass regulations on domestic banks. Since the 2008–2009 crisis, regulators are shifting from LTV-driven standards to DTI-driven ones. The government-sponsored Korea Mortgage Corporation (KoMoCo) issued several MBS collateralized by mortgage exposures, whose origination is subsidized by government funds.
Taiwan, China	Banks	Mainly		
Thailand	Banks and housing finance agencies	Mainly; also government backed bonds	Low	The state-owned financial institution has the largest share.

*The Czech Republic has been reclassified as an advanced economy; it was an emerging economy during the precrisis years.

Note: LTV = Loan-to-value ratio; AHML = Agency for Housing Mortgage Lending.

Source: IMF Global Financial Stability Report, *Durable Financial Stability: Getting There from Here*, April 2011.

Table 4.2   Mortgage Market Characteristics in Emerging and Newly Industrialized Economies (2008)

Country	Government Support					
	Subsidies to First-Time Buyers Up Front	Subsidies to Buyers Through Savings Account Contributions	Subsidies to Selected Groups, Low Income	Provident Funds Early Withdrawal for Housing Purposes	Housing Finance Funds, Govt. Agency Providing Guarantees, Loans	
Brazil	Yes	Yes	Yes	Yes	Yes	
Chile	Yes	Yes			Yes (credit enhancements to lenders)	
China			Yes	Yes		
Croatia		Yes, through Bauspar (15%)				
Czech Republic°°		Yes (Bauspar, up to 15%)				
Hungary		Yes, Bauspar				
India	Yes		Yes, through soft loans		Yes	
Indonesia	Yes		Yes (also to moderate income)		Yes	
Malaysia			Yes, to government employees	Yes	Yes, through Cagamas, but without formal government support	
Mexico	Yes	Yes (savings leveraged to market-based mortgage finance)	Yes	Yes (housing fund)	Yes	
Poland	Yes (limited interest rate subsidies during first eight years of loan)					
Russia			Yes		Yes	

| | | Interest Rate Type | Loan-to-Value Ratio (LTV) | | | |
Tax Deductibility of Mortgage Interest	Capital Gains Tax Deductibility	Majority of the Contracts	Maximum Allowed with Mortgage Insurance	Average	Observed Maximum[a]	For Covered Bonds
		Variable		80–100	100	
		Variable			75	75–100 (depending on the mortgage product)
		Variable		60	80	
Yes		Fixed/variable	75			70
Yes (up to maximum level)		Fixed (mixed)			100	
		Variable (mixed)			70	70 (in 2009)
Yes	Yes, if invested in a second property	Mixed			110	85
		Variable			90	80–90
		Variable			80	90
		Variable			95 (depends on the provider)	
Only for loans originated before 2007 and subject to a cap	Yes (with limits)	Variable			100	
Yes		Fixed/variable		60		85

Table 4.2 Mortgage Market Characteristics in Emerging and Newly Industrialized Economies (2008) (continued)

| Country | Government Support | | | | |
	Subsidies to First-Time Buyers Up Front	Subsidies to Buyers Through Savings Account Contributions	Subsidies to Selected Groups, Low Income	Provident Funds Early Withdrawal for Housing Purposes	Housing Finance Funds, Govt. Agency Providing Guarantees, Loans
Singapore			Yes, through Housing Development Board	Yes	Yes (loan origination)
South Africa			Yes		Yes
South Korea			Yes, through National Housing Fund		Yes (long-term, fixed-interest loans); MBS
Taiwan Province of China	Yes	Yes	Yes		
Thailand	Yes, tax breaks				Yes

* The observed maximum refers not only to published maximum LTV ratio, but also to anecdotal evidence from various sources cited.

** The Czech Republic has been reclassified as an advanced economy; it was an emerging economy during the precrisis years.

Note: MBS = Mortgage-backed securities.

Source: IMF Global Financial Stability Report, *Durable Financial Stability: Getting There from Here,* April 2011.

We next consider the case of China in depth. The transformation of the housing system there from one in which the government provided all housing through employers to a market-oriented one provides a singular example of change and innovation. Also important is the question of whether a bubble exists in Chinese real estate.

Tax Deductibility of Mortgage Interest	Capital Gains Tax Deductibility	Interest Rate Type	Loan-to-Value Ratio (LTV)			
		Majority of the Contracts	Maximum Allowed with Mortgage Insurance	Average	Observed Maximum°	For Covered Bonds
Yes		Variable		<70	80	80–90
		Variable			100	
Yes, up to a maximum		Variable	80	60–70	70	60–70 (40–60 regulatory)
Yes, up to a maximum		Variable			100	
Yes, up to a maximum		Fixed/variable			90–100	70–90 (100 by Government Housing Bank)

China

The IMF predicts that, in 2016, China, the most populous country in the world, will become the largest economy in terms of purchasing power parity (PPP).[2] Housing for China's 1.34 billion people is clearly a cornerstone of its economic activity.

The last 30 years have seen a major change in this dimension. When China had a centrally planned economy, the state provided housing through work units. Over time, the market has gradually replaced this system. The great worry now is that there is a bubble in property prices in at least some parts of the country, and many Chinese are unable to afford housing. In this chapter, we start by considering how China has transformed its system of housing.

Property Prices in China

In a popular television series called *The Snail House*, a young couple struggles to obtain a good apartment to live in. The series is filmed in Shanghai. Hai Ping, the heroine, graduated from one of the best universities in China and works hard in a white-collar job. Her husband, who is also well educated, doesn't make much money. Hai Zao is Hai Ping's younger sister. She helps by borrowing money obtained through corruption from her (older) married lover, Song Siming, who is the secretary to the mayor. He eventually commits suicide while under investigation by the police. The series is a heady mix of sex, wealth, spicy humor, and intrigue.[3] Many young people in Shanghai and other major cities in China can empathize with the struggling characters in *The Snail House*.

Figure 4.2 shows the path of property prices in Shanghai relative to household disposable income. For the first six years, housing prices tracked disposable income except for a small blip upward in April 2005. After this, prices stayed fairly constant as household income caught up with the new level.

At the end of 2008 and beginning of 2009, prices took off relative to disposable income until the end of 2010. This is the "bubble" that many have talked about. At the start of 2011, prices fell sharply before they stabilized, and household income began to catch up again. As we discuss shortly, the fall was perhaps as a result of macroprudential policies that the Chinese government introduced to reduce property prices.

Figures 4.3, 4.4, and 4.5 show the same data for Beijing, Guangzhou, and Shenzhen. For Beijing, house prices tracked disposable income until the end of 2006. They then jumped above income and stayed at a mostly higher level until the end of 2008. In 2009, they rose with a jump at the start of 2010. As in Shanghai, prices peaked at the end of 2010 and then fell sharply at the start of 2011 before stabilizing somewhat.

Figure 4.2   Shanghai housing price versus disposable annual income per capita, normalized and adjusted by CPI, 2002 = 100.

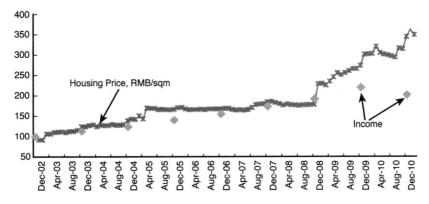

Figure 4.3   Beijing housing price versus disposable annual income per capita, normalized and adjusted by CPI, 2002 = 100.

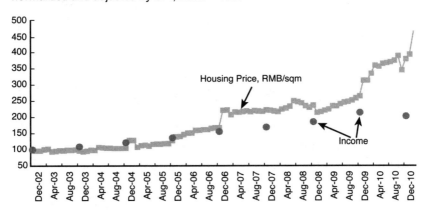

Figure 4.4 Guanzhou housing price versus disposable annual income per capita, normalized and adjusted by CPI, 2002 = 100.

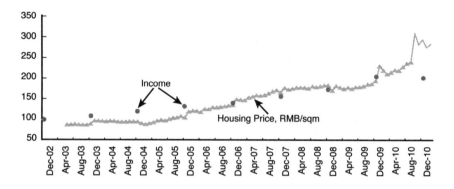

Figure 4.5 Shenzhen housing price versus disposable annual income per capita, normalized and adjusted by CPI, 2002 = 100.

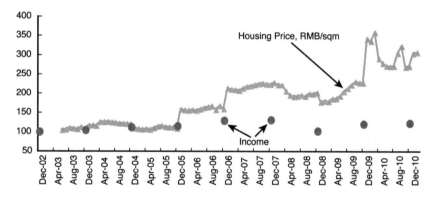

The experience of Guanzhou, shown in Figure 4.4, is different than that of Shanghai and Beijing. Property prices fell behind disposable income until the end of 2006. They then tracked each other fairly closely until the end of 2009. During 2010, there was a dramatic rise and then a fall at the beginning of 2011 before stabilization. Shenzhen had yet another different experience, as shown in Figure 4.5. Here the two series followed each other fairly closely until the end of 2005. But then prices jumped at the start of 2006 and again at the beginning of 2010. After that, they were very volatile.

Figure 4.6 gives the plot of property prices and household disposable income for the country as a whole. You can see that, until 2007, property prices and disposable household income moved together. After that, property prices mostly rose, but not as much as income. This appeared to rule out a bubble in housing prices for China as a whole.

Figure 4.6   National housing price versus disposable annual income per capita, normalized and adjusted by CPI, 2002 = 100.

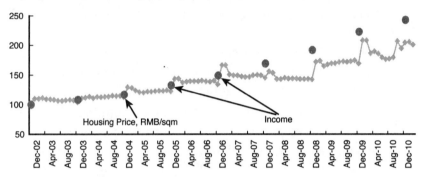

Although that may be true, many argue that there is a bubble in property prices in some of the major cities, such as Shanghai and Beijing.[4] The evidence shown in Figures 4.2–4.6 is crude, as disposable income is just one indicator. However, it does seem that there was a significant rise in prices in a number of property markets in 2010 and then a retrenchment at the start of 2011.

Given the fact that China has the second-largest economy in the world, a housing bubble, if one exists, is a problem not just for China, but also for the rest of the world. We consider a wider range of evidence next.

A Brief History of Housing Provision in China (1949 to the Present)

Soon after the People's Republic of China was founded in 1949, all urban residential units were nationalized. State-owned housing was funded through the annual State Budgetary Funding. Units were allocated to individual households through employers, which were state-owned enterprises (SOEs) or some type of collective or other state-run work unit.[5]

In 1978, the government decided to reform the housing system. The aim of this was to gradually transform the nature of the housing system from a socialist one to a private one. As part of this reform, governments of all levels were to be freed from their housing finance burden and housing shortages were to be alleviated. In 1979, a trial privatization of state-owned residential housing units took place in several coastal cities. The government expanded it in stages until it eventually covered the whole country. The first private housing developer was founded in 1980 in Shenzhen. In the early stages, private-sector housing units were for foreigners and employees of non-state-owned enterprises, but this changed over time.

The key legal change came in 1988. The constitution adopted in 1982 clearly outlawed private ownership of land: "No organization or individual may appropriate land, buy, sell or lease land or unlawfully transfer land in other ways." In 1988, the following sentence was added just after this one: "The right to the use of the land may be transferred in accordance with the law."[6] The maximum term for the transfer of such land-use rights is 70 years for residential property, 40 years for commercial property, and 50 years for industrial and other types of property. Currently, it is not known what will happen with these leases and the structures built on the land when they expire. One possibility is that they will be renewed with another payment to the government or that they will be extended for at least some period in return for payment.

The Chinese system of land-use rights also serves as a partial control on zoning. The differing types of permission limit what can be done with the land. Land-use rights have been sold for only a limited amount of land, and they are not the only control on land use. In addition, the Land Administration Law requires governments at all levels to draw up plans for land use.

During the ten years after the 1998 change in the constitution, a gradual transition took place from the old system to the new private ownership system. Housing units were sold to residents at below-market prices. Work units were required to gradually eliminate their allocation of living units to employees. In 1998, the State Council issued the 23rd Decree, which required work units to stop developing employee housing.

As a result of these changes, the portion of the population living in private-owned or rented housing units went from 9.2% and 6.2% in 2000, respectively, to 16.3% and 12.2% in 2005.

An important part of the transition from state-owned housing is that private housing is supplemented with public housing targeted at low- and middle-income households. These units are rented or bought from local governments at heavily subsidized prices. In recent years, however, the construction of this type of housing fell substantially because of the lack of financial incentives.

Table 4.3 shows that the percentage of affordable housing fell from 21.8% of initiated construction space in 2000 to 5.2% in 2008. Gao (2010) interviewed managers from the largest real estate developer in China, Vanke. The developer explained that the profit for affordable housing was ¥200/m², compared to ¥17,000/m² for townhouses and ¥37,000/m² for single-family homes.[7]

Table 4.3 Total Building Space of Newly Built Residential Houses for Middle- and Low-Wage Earners in the PRC (1997–2008)

Year	Initiated Construction Floor Space (10,000m²)	Initiated Construction for Affordable Housing Floor Space (10,000m²)	Affordable Housing Construction Rate (%)
1997	10,996.60	1,720.60	15.6
1998	16,637.50	3,466.40	20.8
1999	18,797.90	3,970.40	21.1
2000	24,401.20	5,313.30	21.8
2001	30,532.70	5,796.00	19.0
2002	34,719.40	5,279.70	15.2
2003	43,853.90	5,330.60	12.2
2004	47,949.00	4,257.50	8.9
2005	55,185.10	3,513.50	6.4
2006	64,403.80	4,379.03	6.8
2007	78,795.51	4,810.26	6.1
2008	83,642.12	4,336.97	5.2

Source: L. Gao, "Achievements and Challenges: 30 Years of Housing Reforms in the People's Republic of China," ADB Economics Working Paper Series No. 198, Asian Development Bank, 2010.

The central government has tried to force developers to build more affordable housing. For example, in 2006, the central government implemented a "90–70" policy requiring that 70% of the total area in each new housing project be allocated to units of 90m² so that they were affordable. However, developers found ways around these restrictions by, for example, designing adjacent "90–70" units so that they could easily be combined to create luxurious apartments after purchase. Local government officials often helped in such schemes, to stimulate revenue and local growth.

To counter the fall-off in the construction of affordable housing, the Chinese government committed in its latest Five-year Plan to building 36 million new units of low-cost housing by 2015.[8] It remains to be seen whether this will be successful.

Is There a Bubble?

So far, we have considered the relationship between property prices and household disposable income. This is just one indicator of whether a bubble exists. What does a wider range of evidence suggest?

Table 4.4 shows the housing price to per capita net income in the ten largest cities in China, as well as in the U.S., Australia, the U.K., and Canada. It can be seen that house prices are much higher based on this measure than in the four other countries. The lowest ratio in China (20 for Wuhan) is more than twice the next highest ratio for the other four countries combined (9.6 for the Sunshine Coast in Australia). The highest ratio (27 for Xiamen) is four times that of London at 6.9, which is often regarded as one of the most expensive cities in the world in terms of property prices.

Cultural factors partially explain the high price-to-income ratios in China. For example, many young people in China regard owning a home as a precondition to starting a family. Chinese parents are often willing to help in this acquisition. Given the one-child policy that has been in operation in China for many years, this means that up to four incomes can be devoted to saving for an apartment or house. In addition to this kind of cultural factor, the lack of good saving instruments in China contributes to the attractiveness of saving to buy property. Deposit accounts give low interest rates, and the stock market has been risky in recent years.

Table 4.4 Cities with High Housing Price–to–Income Ratio Values (2007–2008)

Rank	PRC° City	PI	United States°° City	PI	Australia°° City	PI	United Kingdom°° City	PI	Canada°° City	PI
1	Xiamen	27.0	San Francisco, CA	8.0	Sunshine Coast	9.6	London	6.9	Vancouver, BC	8.4
2	Beijing	25.4	San Jose, CA	7.4	Gold Coast	8.7	Belfast	6.9	Victoria, BC	7.4
3	Shanghai	24.9	Los Angeles, CA	7.2	Sidney	8.3	Southwest Region	6.8	Kelowna, BC	6.8
4	Tsingtao	24.0	New York, NY–NJ–PA	7.0	Bundaberg	7.2	London Exurbs	6.7	Abbotsford, BC	6.5
5	Hangzhou	23.8	San Diego, CA	5.9	Adelaide	7.1	Aberdeen	5.9	Toronto, ON	4.8
6	Dalian	23.3	Miami, FL	5.6	Melbourne	7.1	Edinburgh	5.5	Calgary, AB	4.8
7	Tianjin	23.2	Boston, MA–NH	5.3	Mandurah	7.0	Wales	5.4	Montreal, QC	4.6
8	Wenzhou	22.5	Seattle, WA	5.2	Wollongong	6.8	West Midlands region	5.2	Saskatoon, SK	4.6
9	Ningbo	21.4	Portland, OR–WA	4.9	Newcastle	6.6	East Midlands region	5.1	Edmonton, AB	4.2
10	Wuhan	20.0	Providence, RI–MA	4.4	Perth	6.4	Perth	5.1	Hamilton, ON	4.0

PI = Price-to-income ratio.

*Based on 2007 per-capita net income (three individuals per household) and 2007 average unit housing price (*China 2008 Year Book*); housing price was calculated assuming a 90m² two-bedroom apartment.

**Based on median household income and median house price data in third quarter 2008, *5th Annual Demographic International Housing Affordability Survey* (available at www.business2.com.au/wp-content/uploads/dhi.pdf).

Source: L. Gao, "Achievements and Challenges: 30 Years of Housing Reforms in the People's Republic of China," ADB Economics Working Paper Series No. 198, Asian Development Bank, 2010.

In our discussion of Figures 4.2–4.5, we examined the increase in house prices in four major cities. Over the years, the quality of housing can change significantly. Economists adjust for these changes using what are known as hedonic price indices. One important issue is the extent to which this kind of adjustment would change our conclusions. In a careful study, Wu, Gyourko, and Deng (2011) produced a constant quality price index for newly built private housing in 35 major Chinese cities from the first quarter of 2000 to the first quarter of 2010 (see Figure 4.7). You can see that house prices nationwide increased substantially on this basis.

Figure 4.7 Constant quality price index for newly built private housing in 25 major Chinese cities (Q1 2000 to Q1 2010).

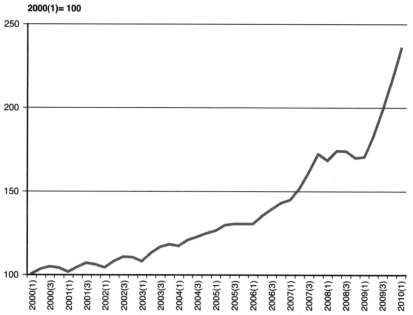

Note: Hedonic models are used to control for quality changes in underlying samples of newly built private homes in 35 major markets in China. Real indices are created by deflating with the CPI series for each market. Aggregate indices are computed as the weighted average of the local market series, with transactions volume between 2000 and 2008 as the fixed weight.

Source: Wu, Gyourko, and Deng (2011), Figure 1.

Wu, Gyourko, and Deng also carefully measured the ratios of the price of properties to the household incomes in that area in eight cities (see Figure 4.8). The price-to-income ratios reached their highest levels in Beijing, Hangzhou, Shanghai, and Shenzhen.[9] Figure 4.9 shows the price-to-rent ratios in the same cities. Hangzhou had the sharpest increase, with the ratio more than doubling, from 31.8 in 2007(1) to 65.5 in 2010(1). The price-to-rent ratio in Beijing increased almost 75%, from 26.4 in 2007(1) to 45.9 in 2010(1). The increase for Shanghai was similar. Shenzhen also had a significant increase. The remaining cities, Chengdu, Tianjin, Wuhan, and Xian, have lower price-to-rent ratios, but these have been increasing over time.

Figure 4.8   Price-to-income ratios in eight major Chinese markets (1999 to Q1 2010).

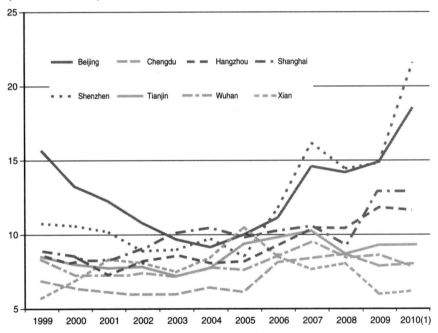

Source: Wu, Gyourko, and Deng (2011), Figure 12.

Figure 4.9   Price-to-rent ratio in eight major Chinese cities
(Q1 2007 to Q1 2010).

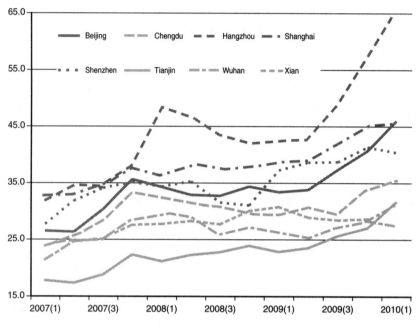

Source: Wu, Gyourko, and Deng (2011), Figure 11.

Based on this and other evidence Wu, Gyourko, and Deng
concluded:

> [M]ultiple parts of the evidence presented in this paper sug-
> gest the potential for substantial mispricing in Beijing and other
> Chinese housing markets. Pricing seems very risky in the sense
> that only modest declines in expected appreciation seem needed
> to generate large drops in house values absent offsetting changes
> in rents or other factors.
>
> The magnitude of the increase in land values over the past
> 2–3 years in particular in Beijing is unprecedented to our
> knowledge. Not only do these increases post-date the Summer
> Olympics, but the recent price surges in early 2010 suggest a
> relationship to the Chinese stimulus package which itself is
> temporary. More broadly, the sharp rises in price-to-rent and
> price-to-income ratios since 2008 in Beijing and many of the
> other large coastal markets look to be very difficult to explain
> fundamentally. (p. 21–22)

In an IMF study, Ahuja, et al. (2010), reached a similar conclusion.[10] They argued that although the evidence suggests no bubble in the country as a whole, some markets, such as Shanghai and Shenzhen, have prices that do seem to be well above fundamentals.

Thus, considerable evidence points to a bubble in some Chinese real estate markets. The drops in prices since the start of 2011 noted earlier may be the first sign of the bursting of the bubble. What may have caused these bubbles? We start with the mortgage finance system and then consider supply and demand factors.

Mortgages in China

It is often suggested that financial innovation in the mortgage market in the U.S. was an important factor in the development of the bubble in the real estate market. The argument is that loosening of underwriting standards, particularly in the subprime market, helped inflate the bubble. Without the innovation of the subprime mortgage, the suggestion is, the bubble would have been mitigated or eliminated.

The case of China provides an interesting example because its mortgage market involves simple, straightforward mortgages.[11] Basic mortgages are 80% or less than the appraisal value or purchase value of the house, whichever is lower. The payment-to-income ratio must be 70% or less. In addition, a requirement states that the ratio of total other assets, including savings accounts, stock market investments, vehicle value, and so forth, to the value of the mortgage should be at least 25%. The term of the mortgage must be 30 years or less, and the sum of the borrower's age and the mortgage term must be 65 years or less.

The interest rates on mortgages in China are adjustable. Mortgages with a term of more than five years are considered long term. The interest rate on them is tied to the six-month bank lending rate set by the People's Bank of China. If this rate changes, mortgage rates are adjusted starting from January 1 of the following year. Short-term mortgages are for five years or less. The interest rate on them is 27 basis points less than on long-term mortgages. Mortgage principal and interest payments can be made by equal or progressive installments.

As the Chinese real estate market boomed in 2007 and 2008 before the demise of Lehman Bros. in September 2008, the Chinese government imposed macro prudential controls, outlined in Table 4.5, to try to limit price appreciation in the real estate market. These involved, among other things, tightening the conditions on mortgages for second and third homes. After the collapse of Lehman Bros. and the slowing of the economy, the government reversed some of the tightening measures on mortgages and introduced supportive measures for the real estate market. After the real estate market started to boom again, the government tightened those measures at the end of 2009. Table 4.5 lists these supportive and tightening measures.

Table 4.5   Property Market-Related Policies in Mainland China

Tightening Measures

Jan 2007	Imposed value-added taxes on land transactions.
Sep 2007	Raised the minimum down payment ratio to 40% and the minimum mortgage rate to 110% of the benchmark rate for a second mortgage. Minimum down payment ratio and mortgage rates are higher for third mortgage loans.
Apr 2008	Imposed tax on capital gains on advanced payments of housing purchases.
Jun 2008	Imposed personal income taxes on corporate purchasing properties for individuals.
Aug 2008	Forbade loans for land purchases and for idle projects.

Supportive Policies

Oct 2008	Waived stamp duty on housing transactions and value-added taxes on land transactions.
	Lowered the minimum mortgage rate to 70% of the benchmark rate and the down payment ratio to 20%.
Dec 2008	Extended preferential policies for first-home purchases to second-home purchases.
	Shortened the housing holding period to enjoy business tax exemption from 5 years to 2 years.
May 2009	Reduced developers' capital requirement for economic and commodity housing investment to 20%.

Tightening Measures

Dec 2009	Extended the housing holding period to enjoy business tax exemption from 2 years to 5 years.
	Required developers to pay at least 50% as the initial payment for land purchase.
Jan-2010	Set minimum down payment ratio for second mortgages at 40%.
Apr-2010	Raised minimum down payment ratio for a first mortgage to 30% for a residential property no more than 90m².
	Raised the down payment ratio for a second mortgage to 50% and raised the minimum rate to 110% of the benchmark rate. The down payment ratio and minimum mortgage rate for the third mortgage and above also were raised.
	Restricted mortgage lending to nonresidents.
	Increased land supply for residential properties.

Note: Some tightening measures launched in September and October 2010 in national and city levels are not displayed in the table. Basically, these measures reinforced those introduced in April 2010. In addition, more than ten major cities (Beijing, Shanghai, Hangzhou, Guangzhou, Shenzhen, Nanjing, Ningbo, Fuzhou, Xiamen, Tianjin, Haikou, and Sanya) set the upper limits of property units that a household can purchase.

Source: A. Ahuja, L. Cheung, G. Han, N. Porter, and W. Zhang, "Are House Prices Rising Too Fast in China?" IMF Working Paper, 2010: 10–274.

Given the simple nature of mortgages in China, it seems that financial innovation has not played a role in the price boom there. The amount that can be borrowed has been strictly limited at 80% of property value or less. Moreover, the mortgages have simple adjustable rates. There are none of the extreme kinds of mortgages, such as subprime loans or mortgages with low teaser rate, that attracted so much criticism in the U.S.

An important difference between China and countries such as the U.S. and the U.K. is the low amount of mortgage debt relative to nominal GDP. Table 4.6 shows that, from 2004 to 2007, the total amount of mortgages in China was about 10% of the GDP. This compares to around 40% in France and Spain and 80% in the U.S., U.K., Australia, and New Zealand. Moreover, the growth rate in China, at 2.4%, was considerably lower than in the other countries. However, in 2008–2009, the growth rate in mortgages, at 16.1%, was considerably higher than in the other countries.

We next consider supply and demand factors that play a role in the property market in China and may have contributed to the bubble.

Table 4.6   Mortgage Market Depth and Growth

	2004–2007		2008–2009	
	Mortgage/ NGDP (%)	Average Growth Rate (%)	Mortgage/ NGDP (%)	Average Growth Rate (%)
United States	76.1	4.2	76.3	
United Kingdom	80.4	5.5	89.4	2.5
France/Spain	42.6	11.5	51.8	4.5
Australia	82.3	5.0	91.8	4.3
New Zealand	81.7	8.7	96.7	4.4
China	10.4	2.4	11.8	16.1

Source: Ahuja et al. (2010), p. 21.

Supply Factors in the Real Estate Market

The ownership structure of land and the way in which it is supplied for residential use is very different in China than in the U.S. and most other countries.[12] In China, the state owns urban land and collectives own rural land. This dual land ownership structure leads to the formation of three types of land markets:

- **The land ownership market.** Also called the land confiscation market, this refers to compulsory acquisition of land sites by the government for public purposes, with reasonable compensation offered to the owners. Confiscation of rural land is the largest part of this market and a source of incremental urban land.
- **The primary market for urban land use rights.** The government sells land-use rights to other parties, and the buyers are allowed to use the sites within a specified period.
- **The secondary market for urban land-use rights.** A buyer acquires land rights in the primary market and then resells these land-use rights to other parties.

The proportion of the population residing in urban areas grew steadily from 20% in 1990 to 45% in 2009. Despite the huge population and the large fraction residing in urban areas, the proportion of land devoted to residential use in China is relatively small: 0.33%, compared to 3.1% in the U.S., for example. As Figure 4.10 shows, the other proportions for land use in the two countries are not that different.

Figure 4.10 Land use in China and the U.S.

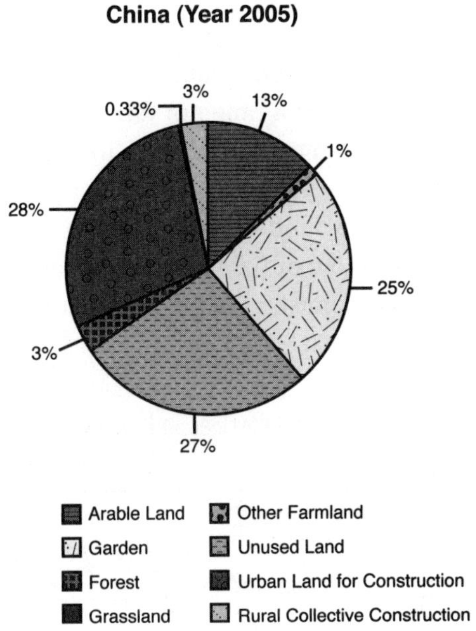
China (Year 2005)
0.33%
3%
13%
1%
28%
25%
3%
27%
Arable Land
Other Farmland
Garden
Unused Land
Forest
Urban Land for Construction
Grassland
Rural Collective Construction

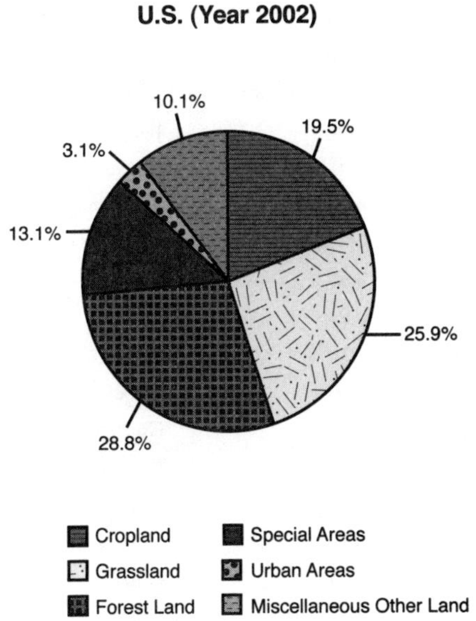
U.S. (Year 2002)
10.1%
19.5%
3.1%
13.1%
25.9%
28.8%
Cropland
Special Areas
Grassland
Urban Areas
Forest Land
Miscellaneous Other Land

Source: National Land Use Planning Outline (2006–2020); Ruben N. Lubowski, "Major Uses of Land in the United States," 2002, from L. Yin, "Is China's Property Market in a Big Bubble?" Working Paper, China Center, Oxford University, 2010.

The other key factor in understanding the supply side of China's real estate market is that local government keeps the revenue from land-transfer fees. This has become a major source of income. Table 4.7 shows the percentage of these land-transfer fees in local GDP and local revenue in 2006 for a range of cities. You can see that the percentage of local GDP ranges from 6.97% for Chongqing to 0.40% for Qinghai, with the average being 3.12%. As a percentage of local government revenue, the land-transfer fees constitute a high of 96.05% for Fujian and a low of 6.04% for Qinghai, with the average being 40.96%. Thus, land-transfer fees represent a substantial revenue source for local governments.

Table 4.7 Percentage of Land-Transfer Fee in Local GDP and Revenue (2006)

Rank	Province	Land Transfer as a Percentage of GDP	Province	Land Transfer as a Percentage of Revenue
1	Chongqing	6.97	Fujian	96.05
2	Fujian	6.83	Zhejiang	77.82
3	Zhejiang	6.42	Sichuan	77.44
4	Jiangsu	5.53	Chongqing	76.62
5	Sichuan	5.45	Anhui	73.29
6	Anhui	5.10	Jiangsu	72.26
7	Liaoning	4.09	Jiangxi	57.54
8	Tianjin	3.82	Hubei	57.08
9	Jiangxi	3.76	Shandong	51.77
10	Shanghai	3.65	Liaoning	46.24
11	Hubei	3.58	Xizang	41.14
12	Guizhou	3.29	Jilin	40.66
13	Shandong	3.18	Tianjin	39.94
14	Ningxia	2.96	Hebei	37.67
15	Guangxi	2.64	Guangxi	37.23
16	Shaanxi	2.63	Hunan	35.88
17	Beijing	2.48	Gansu	34.61
18	Yunnan	2.43	Ningxia	34.32
19	Guangdong	2.35	Guizhou	33.07
20	Jilin	2.33	Shaanxi	32.87
21	Huan	2.27	Henan	30.26
22	Gansu	2.15	Guangdong	28.26
23	Hainan	2.10	Hainan	26.97
24	Xizang	2.06	Yunan	25.66

Rank	Province	Land Transfer as a Percentage of GDP	Province	Land Transfer as a Percentage of Revenue
25	Hebei	2.00	Shanghai	24.03
26	Henan	1.64	Beijing	17.47
27	Shanxi	1.23	Inner Mongolia	16.75
28	Inner Mongolia	1.20	Xinjiang	16.21
29	Xinjiang	1.17	Heilongjiang	14.75
30	Heilongjiang	0.92	Shanxi	9.98
31	Qinghai	0.40	Qinghai	6.04
Average		**3.12**		**40.96**

Source: L. Gao, "Achievements and Challenges: 30 Years of Housing Reforms in the People's Republic of China," ADB Economics Working Paper Series No. 198, Asian Development Bank, 2010.

Because local governments keep the revenue from the land-transfer fees, they have strong incentives to restrict the supply of land and keep the price high. Figure 4.11 illustrates an apparent relationship between the supply of land and the increase in property prices. Thus, supply factors have arguably played an important role in driving property prices higher. Until local government finances are reformed so that they can cover their needs from sources other than land-transfer fees, it seems likely that land supply will continue to be restricted and its value kept higher than would otherwise be the case.

Figure 4.11 Growth of land acquisition area and property prices.

Source: CREIS China Real Estate Index System, from L. Yin, "Is China's Property Market in a Big Bubble?" Working Paper, China Center, Oxford University, 2010.

Demand Factors in the Real Estate Market

The discussion of property prices at the beginning of the chapter suggests there was a significant surge in some places in 2009. Deng, Morck, Wu, and Yeung (2011)[13] argue that this was the result of China's stimulus package that was introduced to counter the effects of the financial crisis. The stimulus package was announced in the fourth quarter of 2008 and amounted to 4.4% of GDP, compared to 4.8% for the U.S. stimulus package. Despite a fall of 44.8% in net exports in 2009, estimated to have cut GDP by 3.9%, Chinese GDP growth on an annualized basis in the four quarters was 6.2%, 7.9%, 9.1%, and 10.7%. The government ordered state-owned banks to lend large amounts. Much of this lending went to large state-owned enterprises (SOEs), as these were regarded as having little credit risk. The SOEs, in turn, spent a large amount of this money in real estate purchases, and this appears to have pushed prices higher. Using data on residential land auction prices from eight major cities, the authors documented that prices rose about 100% in 2009, controlling for quality variation. Moreover, prices rise when SOEs are more active buyers.

Wu, Gyourko, and Deng (2011) also found that SOEs appear to play an important role in driving up land prices. They found a statistically and economically strong positive correlation between land auction prices in Beijing and the winning bidder being a central government–owned SOE. Other factors equal, prices were around 27% higher in this case.

Thus, supply factors were not the only important contributors to the rise in property prices—demand factors were also. In the former case, distortions imposed by the system of local government funding tended to restrict supply. In the latter case, the government's stimulus package nudged prices higher. Although the supply factors are likely to be long lived, the demand factors associated with the stimulus package are not. This also provides part of the explanation for why housing prices fell in some cities at the start of 2011.

The Dangers to the Economy from a Bubble

Given that the financial crisis that started in 2007 originated with the fall of property prices in the U.S. housing markets, an important question for China is how much the Chinese banking system and economy could be hurt by a fall in property prices. We consider this complex issue next.

Gao (2010) points out that real estate developers obtain about 50% of their finance from banks at the national level (refer to Table 4.6). Moreover, in recent years, around 50% of new loans made by banks were residential mortgages (refer to Table 4.7). Although there has certainly been considerable growth in loans to real estate developers and residential mortgages, as Ahuja, et al., point out, the key question is how exposed the Chinese banking system is to a collapse in property prices. They suggest that the direct exposure is low. In late 2009, mortgage loans and loans to developers accounted for less than 20% of total outstanding loans, compared to more than 50% in the U.S. or in Hong Kong.

Although the direct exposure is low, the indirect exposure can be higher because many industries depend on the real estate industry for their demand. For example, the metal smelting and rolling sector, the nonmetal mineral products sector, and the chemical sector are closely linked with the construction industry.

Figure 4.12 summarizes banks' direct exposures and their indirect exposures through industries that rely heavily on construction. Direct exposures of loans to developers and residential mortgages are 18.5% of the total, while real estate dependent industries are 23.8%. Although direct exposures are not high, adding indirect exposures gives significant total exposure.

Finally, Ahuja, et al., point out another indirect exposure: Many loans are secured by real estate collateral. A fall in real estate values means that these loans are no longer guaranteed. The precise impact of this indirect channel is difficult to gauge, however.

The total exposure of the banking system to the real estate sector is difficult to pin down. Combining all the different types of exposure of the banking system to property prices suggests that a sharp fall could undermine financial stability.

Figure 4.12 Distribution of outstanding loans (2009).

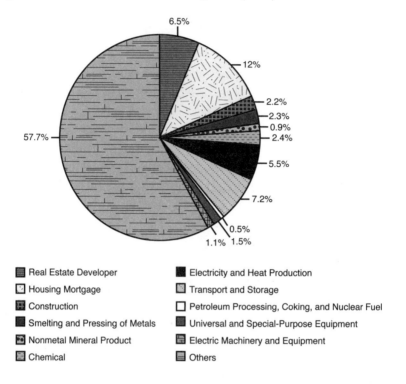

Source: A. Ahuja, L. Cheung, G. Han, N. Porter, and W. Zhang, "Are House Prices Rising Too Fast in China?" IMF Working Paper, 2010: 24.

Endnotes

1 Based on Table 2 from V.C. Warnock and F.E. Warnock, "Markets and Housing Finance," *Journal of Housing Economics* 17 (2008): 239–251.

2 See www.imf.org/external/pubs/ft/weo/2011/01/weodata/index. aspx. The IMF predicts that, in 2016, GDP PPP will be $18,975.744 for China and $18,807.547 for the U.S.

3 See http://blog.sciencenet.cn/home.php?mod=space&uid=54 14&do=blog&id=289449 for a full account of the plot. For excerpts, see www.youtube.com/watch?v=wHsSiCvnNko& feature=related.

4 J. Wu, J. Gyourko, and Y. Deng, "Evaluating Conditions in Major Chinese Housing Markets," forthcoming in *Regional Science and Urban Economics*, 2011.

5 This section draws on Wu, Gyourko, and Deng (2011); G. Stein, "Mortgage Law in China: Comparing Theory and Practice," *Missouri Law Review* 72 (2010): 1,315–1,352; and L. Gao, "Achievements and Challenges: 30 Years of Housing Reforms in the People's Republic of China," ADB Economics Working Paper Series No. 198, Asian Development Bank, 2010.

6 See Stein (2010), p. 1,320–1,321.

7 See Gao (2010), Box 1, p. 9.

8 "Affordable-Housing Delays Threaten China's Economy," *Asian Wall Street Journal,* June 11, 2011.

9 The price-to-income ratios are measured differently than the standard U.S. way, where Price-to-income-ratio = Average total price per housing unit/Average household income, as this data is not available. In the Chinese cities instead:

$$\text{price-to-income ratio} = \frac{\text{average housing price per sq.m floor area} \times \text{housing unit size}}{\text{average per capita income} \times \text{household size}}$$

$$= \frac{\text{average housing price per sq.m floor area}}{\text{average per capita income}} \times \text{housing size per person}$$

See Wu, Gyourko, and Deng (2010) for details.

10 A. Ahuja, L. Cheung, G. Han, N. Porter, and W. Zhang, "Are House Prices Rising Too Fast in China?" IMF Working Paper, 2010: 10–274.

11 The details of mortgages given in this section are based on Y. Deng, D. Zheng, and C. Ling, "An Early Assessment of Residential Mortgage Performance in China," Working Paper, School of Policy, Planning and Development, University of Southern California, 2004; and A. Ahuja (2010). Y. Deng, D. Zheng, and C. Ling, "An Early Assessment of Residential Mortgage Performance in China," Journal of Real Estate Finance and Economics 31 (2005), 117-136.

12 This section draws on L. Yin, "Is China's Property Market in a Big Bubble?" Working Paper, China Center, Oxford University, 2010.

13 Y. Deng, R. Morck, J. Wu, and B. Yeung, "Monetary and Fiscal
Stimuli, Ownership Structure, and China's Housing Market,"
Working Paper, Institute of Real Estate Studies, National Uni-
versity of Singapore, 2011.

5

Future Innovations in Housing Finance

In this chapter, we examine the situation of housing finance in the wake of the mortgage meltdown and global credit crisis, the structural shifts in demand that will drive housing finance innovation in the future, and current supply constraints and attempts to overcome them.

The means and methods of financial innovation for housing are similar for both developed and emerging markets:

- Diversifying sources of capital (debt *and* equity)
- Structuring financial products that will promote private capital investment to return to residential real estate construction, maintenance, and sustainable improvement
- Diversifying types of housing products (single/multiple family)
- Higher-density, sustainable buildings that increase housing consumers' cash flow and ability to service long-term debt
- Pooling savings and risk-management products
- Credit enhancement
- Information technology to monitor and improve efficiency in housing finance

The cascade of foreclosures and defaults, decline of home-ownership, and explosion of "underwater" mortgages overwhelmed both aspiring and existing homeowners in recent years. Home prices have fallen more than 40% since their peak in 2006, one in seven households with mortgages faces foreclosure or default, and nearly 40% of the 48.4 million homes with mortgages are "underwater," meaning that the remaining debt exceeds the value of the property.

The tendency for property prices to fall to the level of foreclosures raises the continued threat of negative equity and a further downward spiral for neighborhoods and local and state governments that must depend on property taxes to support critical services.

Sharing this deep underwater experience that drowned the U.S. housing market are the giant government-sponsored enterprises currently under federal conservatorship, Fannie Mae and Freddie Mac. Acute challenges loom, but they also suggest the way out.

Post-Crisis Housing Markets

Effectively, most of the costs of housing finance risk have been nationalized through the recent crisis. The residential finance system is nearly completely supported by the federal government, a situation that cannot be indefinitely sustained without seriously damaging monetary stability and the prospects for a return to long-term growth. While the financial crisis management led to the recapitalization of large financial institutions, the challenges to revitalize housing finance remain unaddressed, despite green shoots of renewal covered in this chapter.

Until the recent financial crisis, the private sector played a major role in funding residential real estate. Today the way mortgages are originated and sold to the capital markets must be reformed before private capital returns. Most lending institutions held mortgages on their balance sheets, and many investors—domestic and international—bought securities backed by those mortgages. Access to housing finance had grown dramatically and steadily over the preceding decade, and homeownership reached historic highs.

Although the financing of the housing sector remains largely broken, the demographic drivers that will require the return of financial innovation continue unabated. The developed world and emerging markets continue to serve as laboratories for new financial products.

Lending institutions have curtailed credit to the real estate sector as they recapitalize their balance sheets, and investors have cut back on purchases of mortgage-backed securities. The securitization of mortgages by private firms collapsed along with private investor participation. Moreover, most of the funding goes only to the most creditworthy individuals.

This dramatic shift in funding poses a major problem that has yet to be addressed: a growing gap in the availability of credit to residential real estate markets in both mature and emerging markets.

In the U.S., the government has focused on stemming the tide of home foreclosures through loan-modification efforts while also providing its own credit to the housing sector. But this crisis management is not designed to get real estate markets functioning normally again.

Governmental resources are much smaller than those of the global capital markets that must ultimately return to channel investment into housing. Thus, sole dependence on the Federal Reserve and other public entities or GSEs (or similar housing finance agencies overseas) continues to threaten national economic growth and stability. With both major GSEs in conservatorship, the federal government acts as conservator, regulator, and prime investor through the budget (up to $200 billion annually) to keep the housing market liquid. One saying in economics is that trends that can't go on forever won't. This is one of them.

Structural Shifts in Housing Demand

It's important to step back and examine what conditions are brewing to drive the next wave of financial innovation—structural shifts in the demand for capital in housing. By 2010, the ultimate global transition occurred as the majority of the world's population came to live in cities; more than 50.5%, or 3.5 billion people, now reside in urban areas. All future global population growth will occur in urban areas.[1]

By 2030, nearly 60% of the world's population will be urban and more than half will be living in slums. In the developing world, an average five million new urban residents are absorbed in cities each month. Resulting housing shortages are accompanied by increasingly high rates of the depletion of housing stock. Historically, economic growth is always accompanied by decreases in family size, resulting in additional demand for new housing units.

In the U.S., as in many developed countries, immigration drives the majority of population growth. Currently representing 13% of the population in the U.S., immigrants will account for 70% of the population growth and future demand for housing. Their needs, their preferences in housing, and where they locate will drive much housing demand.

Meanwhile, additional age structure and household formation dynamics complicate the demand for capital in housing and need for financing a great portfolio mix of types (single family or multifamily), forms (ownership and rental), and styles (high/low density) emerging in the market.

Younger age cohorts in the population face declining income prospects, with real median household incomes in all age groups under 55 not having increased since 2000. For the youngest working cohorts (25–34), incomes are continuing to fall as they have for the past decade. This trend suppresses household formation due to high unemployment and reduces housing demand in the current period, but accelerates it later as it joins other cohorts in rising demand.[2]

With flat incomes, lost equity in homes, and a declining group of upwardly mobile buyers, housing finance will need to be reinvented. As job creation and economic growth return, housing demand will surge among those who deferred household formation, along with increased needs for single-family and multifamily housing. New entrants in the housing market will require a greater variety of housing options and innovations in finance, construction, and sustainability.

Financial Innovation in Housing: What Works? What Doesn't?

Common to all the innovations we'll examine are answers to some underlying policy questions: What is the structure or preference of tax or other subsidies? What works best, people- or place-based subsidies and incentives? What are the regulatory supply-side constraints in the provision of land and space for development and associated development rights? How can those future construction rights be transferred and ultimately financed? What is the role of information technology in bridging gaps in information about credit analysis, risk, and information concerning housing? How can technology reduce transaction costs and clear the path from savings to investment in housing?

People- Versus Place-Based Subsidies: Policy Successes and Failures in Innovating Housing Finance

Before we examine new waves of financial innovation in housing, it's important to consider some general principles of the incentives that drive housing access and affordability. Tax subsidies, regulatory constraints on property supply through zoning and land-use planning, and technological advances that can bridge information asymmetries in assessing risk should all be considered as elements in the process.

The mortgage interest rate deduction was by far the most prominent feature of tax subsidy for homeownership. From a distributional perspective, the mortgage deduction (as with all deductions) disproportionately favors the wealthy. Although the ownership subsidy has significantly risen over the past 40 years, the rate of homeownership has not varied greatly with those increases. This suggests that the deduction alone has exhausted its ability to subsidize or increase ownership on a sustainable basis.[3]

Although the subsidy contributed to higher demand for larger dwellings (to maximize tax deductibility), increases in total housing stock and its affordability were not maximized through the mortgage deduction. Incentives to maximize deductions through increased leverage and housing size undermined housing sustainability financially and environmentally.

On the other hand, growing evidence indicates that targeted innovations in public policy and financial innovation can increase housing stock and access. Subsidized housing for lower-income residents in many circumstances complements and does not crowd out private investment on a net basis. Government finance raises the total number of units, even with some displacement of privately generated housing. In populous markets, there is less crowding out.

In terms of innovations, the programs that have greatest effect target individual mobility rather than improvement in specific locations. Subsidizing brick-and-mortar building through tax preferences rather than consumers' ability to exercise their own housing preferences leads to outcomes opposite the intended effect of maximizing housing quantity, quality, and choice.[4]

Project-based programs are least effective at subsidizing housing for those who need it. Tenant-based programs that provide certificates and vouchers maximizing choice are most effective in increasing housing stock.[5]

Supply-Side Housing Innovations

An increasing amount of evidence suggests that zoning and other land-use controls contribute to lack of affordability in housing.[6] Zoning restrictions are associated with higher prices by decreasing the available land for construction and development. This suggests that these forms of government regulation contribute to high housing costs.[7]

Reducing implied land-use taxes on new construction has had a considerable impact on housing prices when included in policy innovations. In England, for example, the use of supply-side finance policy demonstrated support for housing affordability through land-use planning.[8]

One key element in nearly all programs is the use of transfer of development rights (TDR). These programs increase housing supply by enabling owners to sell development rights, while encouraging denser residential development in city centers. New development can make an important contribution to housing affordability.[9] The creation and financing of transfer of development rights has been demonstrated in many developing and transitional markets, from India to Russia.

Technology and Financial Innovation

The nexus between information technology and financial product innovation is a pivotal factor. The increasing sophistication of risk estimates, assuming data accuracy and the absence of fraud (two heroic assumptions in the last crisis), enables innovation. The ability to evaluate credit risk and prepayment risk are examples of quantitative pricing, credit scoring, and risk-management systems that are applied to home finance. With lower information processing and communications costs, the activities of back-office mortgage servicers has decreased as service providers extend to geographically dispersed areas.

Credit analysis, with data based on debt payments relative to income, enables more precise measurement of risk. The ability to assign credit scores and automate centralization of credit information can increase access to credit and ability to monitor payments and cash flows at a consumer level. All of this enables greater standardization of documentation and financial structures, which, again, lowers costs.[10]

Financing Housing: Back to the Future

The long-established principles that worked in expanding capital access to the housing industry are the basis of the reinvention of home finance for the future:

- Aligning interests of private capital with policy incentives
- Creating diversified housing stock by eliminating the bias against subsidies for renters
- Pooling savings to create investment vehicles
- Using credit enhancement and guarantees to manage real estate risks
- Creating flexible capital structures for residential developments through structured finance
- Regulating land use to limit supply constraints

The restoration of the historical partnership with private investors will be central to overcoming scarcity in housing access. Because government resources are increasingly limited, bringing back private investment is vital to the return of a vibrant housing finance system.

However, several of the entrenched biases of housing finance will have to be overcome. For one, the overwhelming preference of subsidies to ownership over rental housing has led to rising homeownership accompanied by decreasing affordability. This paradox predictably proved untenable. One hundred percent LTV (loan to value) or negative amortization (interest payments less than the amount owed and added to the loan balance) mortgages were never a sustainable innovation. Along with nonrecourse mortgages and lax regulation, they inflated housing demand while unintentionally creating hidden incentives to default.

Currently, spending programs and tax expenditures (subsidies transferred to consumers or investors through tax reductions) comprise about $300 billion annually. The lion's share of these funds supports homeownership (about $230 billion) over rental affordability (about $60 billion).[11] As a result, homeownership increased to 68% of all households, while the number of households spending more than 30% of their income on housing increased steadily.[12]

To restore the housing sector, the gap between shelter and affordability must be bridged. Favorable tax policies and subsidies are needed for rental housing as well as homeownership, to promote flexibility and choice in housing markets.

Closing the credit gap and moving beyond crisis management are the only ways to restore international investors' confidence in mortgage products in residential single-family and multifamily housing. This requires public *and* private capital. The federal government's dominant role in the real estate markets must be phased out, to free up its resources for other national priorities. Innovations need to focus on restoring

- The role of private investors (domestic and international) as drivers of homeownership and financing
- Confidence in securitization through mortgage-backed securities and covered bonds

Rebooting Structured Finance in Housing

Securitizations, or structured finance products aimed at dispersing risk, must return to basics. Important factors include disclosure transparency, the alignment of interests between mortgage sellers and capital market investors, improvement in collateral quality, and regulatory protections.

A number of measures are being discussed that could contribute to solutions. Financial reform after the crisis created a number of challenges to the resurgence of the mortgage securitization market, including the 5% retention of risk with originating financial institutions. A number of smaller, private-placement mortgage-backed securitizations began to appear over the past year, including one backed by the Federal Deposit Insurance Corporation that included performing loans of 12 failed banks and federal credit enhancement.[13]

More recent transactions have shown that private-sector financing can be done with rates that are within 0.5% of the rates on mortgages financed through government-sponsored enterprises.[14] Nonetheless, the seemingly unlimited extension of the umbrella of Fannie Mae and Freddie Mac crowds out the private market, given the government's access to discounted funds.

The major debate that emerges in how and when securitization can re-emerge revolves around the degree of guarantee the government provides. One proposal has suggested the creation of government-chartered issuers of mortgage-backed securities. These issuers would sell some home loans through government-guaranteed securities. The government-chartered firms would have regulated profitability and fees to cover government guarantees on affordable mortgages and rental housing. This would be an alternative to the almost complete dependency upon government-sponsored enterprises.[15]

Alternatively, others recommend eliminating government guarantees completely and restricting securitization only to the highest-quality mortgages.[16] Issues of affordable housing could then be addressed directly through on-budget social policies rather than the overextension of off-budget guarantees (that eventually find their way back to the federal budget).

Other alternatives or additions to securitization include covered bonds, which are debt securities backed by the cash flows of mortgages that remain on the balance sheet of the issuing financial institutions. These have been effective in Europe and elsewhere but, to date, lack a statutory framework in the United States. Similar to securitization, the covered bond system creates tradable instruments that increase liquidity.

One feature of the Danish model of covered bonds could be helpful in other countries. The capital structure of these bonds enables borrowers to manage risks and mortgage balances as interest rates change. In this model, when a lender issues a mortgage, it is obligated to sell an equivalent bond with a maturity and cash flow that exactly match the underlying home loan. The issuer of the mortgage bond remains responsible for all payments on the bond, but the mortgage holder can buy back the bond in the market and use it to redeem the mortgage and deleverage household balance sheets when interest rates rise and home prices fall.[17] This ability to manage interest-rate risk and credit risk reduced the waves of defaults and foreclosures in other countries and could do so in the U.S. as well.

From Crisis to Innovation: Working out the Foreclosure Crisis

As we've seen historically, innovation usually emerges from new necessities created by crisis and scarcity. A good way to see the beginnings of the next wave of financial innovation is to work through the problems created by the overhang of foreclosed properties from the mortgage meltdown.[18]

The U.S. averaged more than 70,000 home repossessions per month since the crisis. The crisis created a demand for ways to buy and rehabilitate properties that had entered foreclosure, failed to sell at auction, and were owned by mortgage lenders. This real-estate-owned (REO) inventory expanded in recent years from government-sponsored enterprises as well.

These properties, which remained vacant as supply outstripped demand, represented a resale inventory glut of 13.9 million homes by 2009, roughly 11% of all housing units and considerably more than housing vacancies in previous recessions. Housing markets and neighborhoods would benefit if investors were able to buy and rehabilitate these properties and turn them into long-term affordable housing or rental units.

Financing is needed to address these challenges. The structural demand for capital includes

1. Short-term capital to acquire property
2. Midterm needs to rehabilitate or demolish homes
3. Exit financing to transfer property to a buyer

At the same time, operational capacity to handle the flood of foreclosed and defaulted properties is reduced. This demands innovative pricing models that can aggregate capital sources to clear the logjam of foreclosed properties while maintaining ways to make those residences affordable. Let's consider these various dimensions of financial innovation in turn.

Innovative Pricing Models

In markets where values are fluctuating, it is important to find ways to arrive at a fair, affordable price. Two innovative models have emerged from the crisis to deal with this problem:

- **Top-down approach.** The National Community Stabilization Trust (NCST) starts with a market price under normal conditions and then derives a current value. It calculates a "net realizable value" by starting with the estimated market value and subtracting holding, insurance, and other market-specific costs. Key to this approach is that the final sale price reflects local market conditions and predictions about future home prices.
- **Bottom-up approach.** The Community Asset Preservation Corporation (CAPC) of New Jersey buys pools of nonperforming mortgages and REO properties in low- and moderate-income communities. The CAPC then employs a variety of strategies to return these properties to productive use. Its pricing model starts with an estimate of current value and adds the costs necessary to bring the property to market. In March 2009,

CAPC was the first nonprofit to complete a bulk purchase of foreclosed properties.

In both cases, the focus is on underwriting a borrower (rather than the property) into an affordable mortgage and thereby forcing a write-down of property value to the point that negative equity would be reversed. By working with private funds that bought marked-down mortgages, the ability to create realistic values emerged.

Clearing the Property Logjam

Another important innovation has been setting up intermediaries between REO servicers and local housing organizations, nonprofits, or governmental agencies seeking to stabilize neighborhoods and alleviate collapsing values. For example, in 2008, some of the country's largest community development organizations—Enterprise Community Partners, Housing Partnership Network, Local Initiatives Support Corporation, and NeighborWorks America—came together to form NCST. Today the National Urban League is also part of the effort.

The nonprofit's goal is to act as a bridge between state and local housing providers and the REO departments within financial institutions, which are typically not accustomed to working together. NCST facilitates the transfer of foreclosed properties to local and community development organizations.

In addition, the NCST provides flexible capital to help communities leverage their Neighborhood Stabilization Program funds and finance state and local acquisition efforts, builds local capacity through organizing and facilitating collaboration and engagement with the Trust's partners, and acts as an industry voice for neighborhood stabilization.

Aggregating Capital

After the financial crisis, Neighborhood Stabilization Program, part of the Housing and Economic Recovery Act, provided down payment assistance and credit enhancement to leverage private capital by allocating $3.92 billion to state and local governments and nonprofits focused on housing. Obviously, this amount could address only a small portion of REO properties.

Until housing markets recover, public subsidies and philanthropic capital must leverage private capital to have a widespread impact. Creative financing is necessary at each stage, from the acquisition of the properties to disposition.

Some strategies for aggregating capital might include

- **Use program-related investments (PRIs).** PRIs, below-market investments, could be used more widely to subsidize returns for private capital. With public subsidies and dollars from socially motivated investors, PRIs could take the form of subordinated debt as an external credit enhancement.
- **Credit-enhance housing funds.** Government dollars could also be used for credit enhancement. Protecting private-sector investments from the downside would encourage investors.
- **Create a publicly traded investment vehicle.** A publicly traded tax-advantaged vehicle for foreclosure acquisitions would be able to raise large amounts of private capital to stabilize communities.
- **Allow specialized asset managers.** New mortgage and securitization paradigms are essential. By creating safe harbors for specialized asset managers, who would be allowed to make decisions on loan modification without fearing litigation from investors and have a greater authority in administrating the pool of loans, new investors could be brought in to meet stronger underwriting regulatory standards.
- **Increase access to takeout financing to retire existing short- or long-term debt on more favorable terms.** Access to responsible takeout financing is essential to put individuals in homes they can afford by retiring and refinancing existing mortgages on more favorable and sustainable terms. One example is the model successfully used by Neighborhood Assistance Corporation of America in low- and moderate-income communities. NACA developed and uses online software that features a user-friendly application process and stores a borrower's documents. This greatly facilitates the underwriting of mortgages and enables NACA to offer a 30-year, fixed-rate product at a slightly below-market rate

with no down payment and no closing costs. Only 0.0023% of homeowners who bought this product defaulted on their mortgages. In addition, NACA holds free events around the country to restructure unaffordable mortgages.[19]

Preserve Affordability

Innovative financial products can help low- to moderate-income households achieve the dream of homeownership more safely than the mortgage products that failed in recent years. Excessive leverage without equity sponsorship or equity support created capital structure and financial products that were likely to fail.

Negative equity, nonrecourse loans, and declining markets combine to create an incentive for borrowers to default. The most promising counter to the problems of inadequate equity is, well, more but different equity. Financial options such as lease-purchase mortgages and shared-equity mortgages have emerged that provide a middle ground between rental and ownership. They are especially attractive for households that cannot initially qualify for standard mortgages but could be candidates for homeownership several years down the road.

- **Shared-equity ownership.** Models of shared equity, such as deed-restricted housing, community land trusts, and limited-equity cooperatives, are time-tested in the U.S. and Europe. A government or nonprofit invests in a property alongside the homebuyer. Shared equity enables borrowers to trade some potential upside of a purchase for financing. Hundreds of these programs now operate in the U.S.

- **Lease-to-purchase mortgages.** Self-Help is piloting this more experimental solution. The nonprofit buys and rehabilitates properties in Charlotte, North Carolina, and then leases the homes to "tenant purchasers," renters likely to be able to assume Self-Help's lease-purchase mortgages in one to five years. During the rental period, Self-Help provides credit and homeownership counseling and property-management services, to the tenant purchasers. When the tenant purchaser qualifies, he or she assumes the lease-purchase mortgage from Self-Help.

Rental Housing

Rental housing has been largely ignored as part of federal housing policy. As noted earlier, rental housing represents less than a third of the tax subsidies and expenditures provided for homeownership.[20] This is especially true as it relates to low-income rental housing, where the amount spent on assistance declined both as a percentage of nondefense discretionary spending and as a share of GDP. Rental vacancy rates hover at their highest levels (8%) since 1980, and multifamily starts are down two-thirds from their peak two years ago.

The demand for new rental housing is increasing, due to high levels of immigration, lower incomes, and delayed workforce and housing market entry by younger consumers.

Aside from homeless assistance, all categories of low-income housing assistance for renters have declined in recent years, including Section 8 rental assistance through public–private partnerships, housing choice vouchers that encouraged tenant mobility, and public housing. Clearly, structured finance products that address this growing demand for rental housing and developers will emerge.

Housing in Developing Countries

Housing loans comprise a very small amount of total credit in low-income countries. According to the World Bank, only 3% of outstanding credit is in housing in low-income countries, compared to 27% in high-income countries.

The developing world has among the lowest outstanding mortgage debt as a percentage of GDP—3% in Bangladesh, 7% in India, 15% in China, and 17% in Thailand, compared to 42% in the European Union.[21] The overwhelming majority of the population in developing nations does not qualify for mortgage finance.[22]

Most countries face accumulating housing shortages through increased demand driven by rapid urbanization. The formal housing sector provides only a minority of the housing stock. The urban housing backlog is 25 million units in India and 3 million units in Pakistan. High percentages of housing stock require replacement and additions in Afghanistan, Egypt, and throughout the developing world. The informal sectors provides from 60% to 80% of all housing stock.[23]

Underlying all issues is the proper functioning of property markets and property rights to facilitate housing finance. As Hernando DeSoto has shown, the problem is the existence of "dead capital" that cannot be monetized in the market. He has shown that the value of savings in land is huge multiples of the amount received in foreign direct investment, yet the ability to finance those assets lags because of the absence of effective private property rights and markets.[24]

The length of time it takes to obtain authorization or register land creates overwhelmingly high transaction costs that block the use of land and housing property as collateral to access credit for development. Poor information systems are also a hindrance. Associated with these limitations is the absence of long-term credit, meaning that property assets, which are long term, are mismatched to the assets they must finance. Short maturities, high transaction costs, ineffective legal and judicial systems, and the reluctance of the formal sector to enter poor markets limit the ability to solve housing problems in the developing world.[25]

Common to all the emerging models of housing finance innovation are several demonstrated patterns. The attempt to build and maintain lower price points for housing access requires public–private partnerships, which have been more successful than public housing agencies that had limited term and capacity.[26] Leveraging funds through public–private partnerships have made programs more sustainable. Purely public programs were more open to corruption and abuse. Linkages to large-scale builders, building associations, and conventional commercial banks under conditional, performance-based terms have improved delivery of housing finance. Transparency and restrictions on sales for specific terms have prevented speculation. Encouraging ownership, joint guarantees (additional security through microfinance structures to ensure repayment), and cross-subsidy models have increased the flow of housing credit.[27]

Savings Models

In most rapidly growing Asian economies, some of the most promising models seek to encourage and leverage consumer savings to drive housing finance. Compulsory and contractual savings schemes to provide a capital base for housing investment have proliferated. In both China and Singapore, successful housing finance models include mandatory housing provident funds. Employers and employees contribute a matching percentage of salary for housing-related expenses, including down payments, monthly payments, and building repairs.

Borrowings from the housing provident funds can be advanced for homeownership and leverage additional bank loans. Funds not used for housing are returned at retirement. China allows for a 5% contribution from employees and employers to build the housing fund.[28]

In Singapore, the provident fund embeds lifetime earnings for retirement and channels it toward housing by allowing a household to borrow up to 20% of its retirement fund. Appreciation can accrue toward repayment of those loans on a deferred basis upon realization.[29]

Australia also has innovative mechanisms matching access to retirement funds for households with permanent jobs to long-term housing assets. Pension funds can provide additional cash that low- and moderate-income families can apply to down payments and mortgages. The use of pension fund savings can lower carrying costs substantially and increase the capacity of homeowners to support mortgage debt.[30]

Land Trusts

Renewable, long-term leaseholds are made available through land trusts held by nonprofit housing corporations or cooperatives for development. These land trusts or land banks enable nonprofits or governments to acquire, preserve, convert, and manage foreclosed and other vacant and abandoned properties. By permitting the relevant agency (public or nonprofit) to aggregate and obtain title to these properties, a usable asset is created to reduce blight, generate revenue, and facilitate affordable housing by lowering land acquisition costs and aggregating parcels for development.[31]

Organizational Innovations

Although housing has occupied a relatively small niche of microfinance, some microfinance institutions have expanded into the sector. In South Asia and Latin America, nonprofit microfinance institutions have joined government and private for-profit and nonprofit organizations as co-investors. By linking banks, housing agencies, and individual consumers, intermediaries can provide loans for housing rehabilitation, new homes, resettlement, and infrastructure.[32]

Microfinance institutions (Grameen, Banco Sol, MiBanco), nongovernmental organizations (Accion, FINCA), cooperatives, mutual savings associations, municipalities, government housing programs, and commercial banks have joined together to downscale lending, create new securities and guarantees, mobilize data technology for tracking credits, and mobilize credit enhancement to reduce lending risks.[33]

Housing Bonds

Mortgage banks have used long-term housing bonds to mobilize funds for housing finance. Where tax exemption has been deployed for these instruments, mortgage banks can lower their cost of capital by issuing bonds at below-market interest rates. Housing agencies have issued bonds for mortgages on apartment rentals and owner-occupied housing. Housing agencies issuing the bonds fund private-lending institutions that provide mortgages at a lower cost.[34]

Revolving Loan Funds

Revolving loan funds operate through a variety of organizational forms (government, NGOs, and public–private partnerships in conjunction with commercial banks or nonbank lenders). The purpose of these funds is to provide long-term, self-sustainable sources of finance to build and upgrade housing based on initial capitalization of the funds (through government and nonprofit foundation funds) and driven by interest and repayment revenues. Under these funds, deficits are covered by drawdowns from accounts and interest charges. Loans can be disbursed by stages of construction and performance. In many cases, they are available for construction and home improvement and offer flexible conditions and options regarding repayment.[35]

Credit Enhancement

Credit enhancement, the ability to cushion or protect against loan losses, has a long history and an important future in housing finance innovation. By dispersing risk of loss, either through internal measures provided by the borrower or by government, philanthropic, or other outside entities, these measures can extend credit access.

Credit enhancement provides a form of insurance that reduces the risk of loss based on detailed credit analysis. The mortgage originator provides internal credit enhancement within subordinated layers of the capital structure and the structure of loan payments. Reserve accounts to ensure against default risk are funded by excess interest rate spread payments (larger than the amount needed for debt servicing), over-collateralization (holding assets of greater value than the debt issued), and additional debt coverage. Outside parties, bank letters of credit, private or public insurance, additional guarantees or collateral pledged, or subordinated loans from other parties can provide external measures.[36]

In all these cases, loan losses are covered by enhancement pools covering a certain portion of the outstanding debt, thereby ensuring the extension of additional credit risk. The adaptation of these measures to a variety of situations by governments, multilateral organizations, philanthropies, and financial institutions has been increasingly widespread.

Sustainable Housing, Sustainable Financial Innovation

The rising demand and costs of housing will drive innovation that is environmentally and financially sustainable. As several recent studies have demonstrated, savings in the costs of homes through suburbanization are being offset by unsustainable costs in transportation and energy.[37] As prices decline in the peripheral areas of major metropolitan centers, many new or displaced homeowners will continue to leave behind the communities in which they work and commute greater distances.

However, the growing costs of transportation and other services will more than offset the savings in home costs. As John McIlwain has pointed out, "[T]he outer suburbs will have the least expensive housing, but the cost in time and money of long commutes will eliminate any savings."[38]

The importance of financing infrastructure and housing in transportation-oriented development will increase in response to pressures to improve workforce productivity and avoid the productivity losses caused by congestion.

New modes of development favor increasing population densities and reurbanization to create market mechanisms that respond to challenges of sustainable energy and transportation costs and environmental sensitivity.[39] New studies show that, in more than half of the U.S. metropolitan areas, new residential building permits, density, and revitalization have dramatically increased. Infill development that uses land within built-up areas becomes more significant.

Residential and commercial buildings account for almost 40% of the greenhouse gas emissions in the U.S. With Americans spending approximately 90% of their time indoors, it is clear that green building is the direct path to a cleaner and healthier future.

Increasing energy efficiency while decreasing the catastrophic effects of the burning of fossil fuels, green building also represents an important opportunity to generate new jobs and promote economic growth. A 2008 study by the Lawrence Berkeley National Laboratory of Science estimates that a reasonable level of nationwide energy-efficiency upgrades, costing $22 billion per year, would result in nearly $170 billion in annual savings.[40] Given the political shift toward "going green," now more than ever, there is real momentum to significantly change construction in this country.

Before the current economic crisis, the green building growth rate was about 50% to 75% per year, representing about 5% of new construction. Around the country, there are 5,000 LEED- and ENERGY STAR-certified commercial buildings, with 800,000 ENERGY STAR homes and approximately 2,000 Green-point rated homes. However, significant capital is needed to scale the retrofitting of residential, commercial, industrial, and retail properties. And although preliminary financing models have seen relative success with individual pilot projects, long-term, large-scale innovations need to be refined to create sustainable sources of funding. From the municipal bond market to green building securities, leveraging investment from the capital markets will ensure a more effective use of public and private resources.

A broad array of green building and other sustainable finance products is beginning to appear, including

- Direct mortgage, construction, and rehabilitation loans for residential properties
- Structured finance products that monetize cash flows from energy efficiency and environmental savings
- Pooled green real estate debt and equity funds and investments
- Insurance and asset-management products and services for green buildings to monitor and capitalize energy efficiencies[41]

The objective of these measures would be to reduce risk and create higher-valued collateral, create a cheaper cost of capital and enhanced liquidity for environmental efficiencies in homes, and provide underwriting standards for assets to be financed in this growing market.

Financing Energy and Environmental Efficiencies[42]

We have long known that energy efficiency is the cheapest source of power. But our ability to implement solutions has been hindered by high upfront costs and uncertainty about benefits. A number of innovative financing models and program delivery have emerged in recent years that will certainly expand in the future.

Currently, there are 130 million homes in the United States—and their combined energy demand accounts for 20% of the nation's greenhouse gas emissions. Studies have consistently found that nationwide energy-efficiency upgrades would significantly reduce emissions, create green jobs, and pay for themselves. According to "Recovery through Retrofit," a recently released White House report that lays the groundwork for building a sustainable home-retrofit industry, existing techniques and technologies can reduce energy consumption by up to 40%, potentially saving $21 billion annually in home energy bills.[43]

Greening older buildings has become a top priority for the U.S. Department of Energy and the White House. The availability of multibillion-dollar funding from the federal stimulus package (the American Recovery and Reinvestment Act of 2009, or ARRA) has paved the way for programs aimed at improving residential energy efficiency.

The DOE has issued a request for proposals for a new Retrofit Ramp-Up initiative, specifically seeking "game-changing" programs. It has encouraged state and local governments to create financing mechanisms that can leverage public money to drive the broader adoption of retrofits. President Obama has also proposed the HOMESTAR program, which would help households pay for retrofit projects, reducing their high initial costs.[44]

Stimulus funding represents the largest injection of federal dollars for energy efficiency in U.S. history. But given the enormous cost of comprehensively retrofitting millions of homes, even these record sums are insufficient. It is therefore crucial to use these public funds in such a way that private investors are given an incentive to deploy their capital as well.

Residential energy-efficiency financing programs have existed for years in states and municipalities—but so far, none has caught on widely enough to attract private capital. Taking a retrofitting program to scale requires improvement in several areas: marketing of products and services to likely customers; a trained workforce capable of extensive, quality field implementation; financing offers that are replicable; and the ability to sell loan pools into a national secondary market, allowing for a more rapid and systematic recycling of funding back into loan programs.

Furthermore, there is an inherent tension in the need to tailor programs to local conditions and preferences—thus yielding multiple, relatively small loan programs—and the need for large, homogenous pools of securities that can capture the transaction efficiencies of modern financial markets. State and local governments, the administrators of most of the energy-efficiency financing programs, design programs to meet their region's needs but look to access to broader pools of private capital.

Market growth depends on successfully integrating program design and financial product design. Program rules shape the risk/return tradeoff that drives the financial products. Consumers respond to program features such as ease of billing or attractive payment terms, but these details vary considerably across smaller, locally focused programs. Broad standardization is needed for national loan pools and securitization (which would lower costs).

Energy-Efficiency Mortgages

The financial logic of these "green mortgages" is clear: Potential borrowers add the cost of the energy-efficient home improvements to the new mortgage, and the energy savings boosts their disposable income, creating higher borrowing capacity. Energy-efficient mortgages (EEMs) are based on the principle that energy savings create disposable income—and, thus, the ability for a homeowner to carry a larger mortgage to finance these capital improvements. Because the homeowner is presumed to have higher credit quality than otherwise, in theory, the mortgage carries a lower default risk and can be issued at a lower interest rate. EEMs allow homeowners to pay for the cost of energy-efficiency upgrades with tax-advantaged mortgage interest rates, while avoiding large upfront out-of-pocket costs and aligning payments with the long periods it may take for some of the energy-efficiency upgrades to pay off.

Only 1,066 FHA-insured EEMs were originated in the United States in 2007. The numbers in previous years were even lower. Three challenges have emerged. First, the link between energy savings and lower default rates has not been proven, so it is unclear whether the energy savings are sufficient to make it worthwhile for lenders to reprice the loans. Second, the loans are more difficult to sell into the secondary markets, increasing lender risk. Finally, because EEMs are more complicated loans, they are more difficult to make, but lenders have little incentive to offer EEMs because they get no additional compensation for the extra work.

The marketing of EEMs should be easy because homeowners know how to obtain a mortgage and refinance, so the lender can simply introduce energy efficiency into the transaction. Furthermore, the mortgage market infrastructure is huge and efficient, with very low transaction costs. The EEM has been available in all 50 states for more than a decade. Currently, EEMs are sponsored by the FHA, Fannie Mae, the Department of Veterans Affairs, the Agriculture Department, and state housing finance agencies.

Several solutions to the product's design flaws are based on lessons learned. Key provisions include creating an inexpensive, nationally available audit tool to reduce customer costs; qualifying borrowers based on credit risk rather than projected savings; and reducing the cost to the customer and to the lender by using federal and state programs to drive down the interest rate.

Given the potential energy savings, a federal, state, or Fannie Mae/Freddie Mac subsidy to reduce costs in the early years while performance data is gathered would make sense. Pilot programs offering ENERGY STAR–branded mortgages are currently underway. If EEMs reach sufficient volume, performance will be demonstrated and loans can be priced for the secondary market.

Any lender can use the ENERGY STAR mortgage as long as the product meets two conditions. First, it must produce at least a 20% improvement in the whole home's energy use. Second, because the ENERGY STAR brand helps lenders with marketing, lenders must provide consumers with some additional benefit, such as covering the cost of the audit or the appraisal or reducing the interest rate. The pilot programs will demonstrate whether these features increase consumer adoption.

Unsecured Home Improvement Loans

When heating and cooling systems fail and must be replaced, homeowners can often obtain unsecured home improvement loans through the contractor to pay for the replacement. If contractors could refer them to loans offered by different financial institutions (with more choices and made cheaper through subsidies), the consumers' replacement decisions would more likely tip toward energy-efficient systems. Capital to support unsecured home improvement loans for greater energy efficiency comes from public and private sources (including Fannie Mae, state and local budgets, and banks). Several examples include

- **Public loan programs.** Widely available through partnerships with utilities and local banks, the Fannie Mae Energy Loan is the largest public source of unsecured loans. After originating a loan, the Fannie Mae–approved lender transfers loan obligations to Fannie Mae but continues to service the loan. It is the one of the few loan programs with a functioning secondary market at this time. However, it will be challenging to expand, as the interest rate is high (currently between 12% and 15%).

- **Pennsylvania's Keystone Home Energy Loan Program (HELP).** Homeowners receive loans for energy-efficient home improvements at attractive terms in a program provided and subsidized by the state. The state administers the program and acts as a secondary market, buying loans from lenders through its pension funds. By acting as a ready buyer, the state secures the availability of residential home improvement lending and lowers the interest rate offered to consumers.

Although it might be expected that delinquencies and defaults would be a key challenge for these programs, loan loss rates have been very low and have risen only slightly during the recession. The reason? Self-selection by borrowers, who are largely homeowners with no plans to move, great credit scores, and high home equity values. EnerBank reports a ten-year loss rate of only 0.8%, with a small but manageable rise in 2008 and 2009. There is little need for a secondary market partner because so many loans are paid off in the first year.

Although funds for unsecured loans are constrained by the current credit crisis, a large and efficient infrastructure for processing and securitization already exists. Contractors sell the loans as part of their offerings, banks originate the loans, and the secondary markets securitize them as part of ABS financings. Infrastructure for origination and distribution of these loans and a strong base of expertise are already in place. A tiered interest rate to attract proactive buyers, with the best rates reserved for comprehensive home performance loans, appears to have a good track record. With access to a broader secondary market, these programs could grow.

Property Tax–Based Financing

Municipalities have long used property assessments and taxes to finance public projects. Property tax–based financings could also provide homeowners with funding for energy-efficient improvements and solar installations. The homeowner repays the loan through a voluntary increase in the property tax bill. Funds are provided by a local bond mechanism (similar to a municipal bond issued for a specific purpose but are taxable at the federal level). Repayment terms are long (10–20 years), and because repayment is tied to the tax bill and carries the same seniority over the mortgage, default rates should be generally low. Any property assessments in arrears have a senior lien to mortgage payment in the event of default, which led to a Federal Housing Finance Agency directive not to underwrite mortgages for properties with an energy-related assessment. Current litigation and proposed legislation seek to overcome these concerns through Department of Energy and other certifications to ensure that savings could be supported and would serve the interests of building owners, municipalities, and mortgage lenders.

Because basic efficiency measures can cut energy costs by up to 35% annually, energy savings are believed to exceed the cost of related tax assessment, thereby overcoming the upfront cost barrier by financing over a longer term and improving cash flow for owners.[45] When regulatory and legal issues are addressed, similar options will most certainly materialize to address the needs of this financing and overcome the objections of federal regulators.

The loan obligation moves to the next owner if the home is sold. In theory, the energy savings would be greater than the increase in property tax, generating a positive cash flow to the homeowner.

The pool of loans is not tax exempt at the federal level, so it cannot be sold into the tax-free municipal bond market. This decreases liquidity significantly because the tax-free segment of the overall market totals $600 billion per year, while the taxable segment is $6 billion per year. Additionally, the lack of an active securitization market limits liquidity. When the secondary markets do open, government agencies and philanthropic funds could provide credit enhancement to pools of loans, enabling purchase at lower risk.

As a voluntary property tax increase, this type of financing is designed to take seniority over an existing mortgage. New mortgages can be issued with this seniority clearly spelled out, but seniority status for existing mortgages has been challenged. It is not a matter of simply getting the mortgage lender to agree to a change in status. Most mortgages are not held by the original lender, but have been placed in securitized loan pools held by a large number of investors. Financial institutions holding large mortgage pools are very concerned about losing their senior position. Legal opinions vary on this, and the issue has not been resolved.

Sixteen states have passed legislation for these property tax–based programs, allowing municipalities to create financing districts. Pilots have been launched in California (Sonoma County, Berkeley, and Palm Desert); Babylon, New York; and Boulder, Colorado. In these programs, home loans have been financed out of general obligation funds, so the market's acceptance of these new financial products has not been tested. Homeowner acceptance has been good, but project scale to date has been small in each locale. The White House included property-based finance as a major component of the Recovery Through Retrofit plan. The California Energy Commission has funded expansion of PACE throughout California with its allocation of the ARRA funds for energy efficiency.

Whether administered by local government or by an outsourced administrative partner (such as the startup company Renewable Funding), the key bottleneck is transfer of loans from the originator to the secondary markets. An early aggregator and buyer of bonds would resolve a key risk. The use of credit enhancement by the federal government, or possibly state and local government, is needed for property-backed bonds to be placed in the secondary market. Private markets are not currently in a position to provide this insurance, but such bonds may have strong appeal to new lenders because they are secured by tax liens and have seniority to mortgage debt, pending expected legislative resolution of the issues surrounding these innovations. In any case, the ongoing attempt to link long-term asset development to improve energy/environmental efficiency will continue in the future.

One large investment required by the Oregon program was a unified software platform for loan origination and processing. This platform works for three utilities. It is hoped that access to loan payment history, the best predictor of default risk, will help with underwriting and servicing. The platform is intended to become a regional demonstration project.

Conclusion

With national, state, and local governments facing budget crises in the U.S. and Europe, and the overwhelming challenges of growth in the developing world, several common patterns emerge in the range and rate of financial innovation in housing. Governments seek leverage and homeowners seek to manage debt loads to obtain shelter and improve it. Environmental and energy demands link housing to other aspects of physical infrastructure (transportation and communication), social capital (education and community stability), and growing structural demands for capital. The successes outlined here are up and running through long-term financing mechanisms, structured finance, home equity and improvement loans, payment systems, and risk-management software and platforms that help improve credit analysis. Identifying and replicating the best models will work. Different financing programs share many commonalities—credit enhancement and loan loss reserves, diffusion of risk, and program and financial product design that align incentives for the long-term goal of attracting private capital. Tax-advantaged financial innovations promote and enable public–private collaboration by property owners, renters, financial institutions, and growing capital markets that will support expanded access to shelter. Active investment utilizing this financial toolkit will restore shelter access and affordability.

Endnotes

1 "2009 Revision of World Urbanization Prospects," United Nations, March 2010.

2 "2009 State of Nation's Housing," Joint Center for Housing Studies, Harvard University, 2010.

3 Edward L. Glaeser and Jesse M. Shapiro, "The Benefits of Home Mortgage Interest Deduction," NBER Working Paper 9284, October 2002; James Poterba and Todd Sinai, "Tax Expenditures for Owner-Occupied Housing: Deductions for Property Taxes and Mortgage Interest and the Exclusion of Imputed Rental Income," Zell-Lurie Real Estate Center, Wharton School Working Paper, January 2008.

4 Witold Rybczynski, "How Affordable Is Affordable Housing?" Zell-Lurie Real Estate Center, Working Paper 497, December 2010.

5 Todd Sinai and Joel Waldfogel, "Do Low Income Housing Subsidies Increase Housing Consumption?" NBER Working Paper No. 8709, January 2002; Ellen Seidman and Jennifer Tescher, "From Unbanked to Homeowner: Improving the Supply of Financial Services for Low-Income, Low-Asset Customers," Joint Center for Housing, Working Paper Series, February 2004.

6 For example, see William K. Jaeger, "The Effects of Land-Use Regulations on Property Values," *Environmental Law* 36, no. 105 (2006): 105–130.

7 Edward L. Glaeser and Joseph Gyourko, "The Impact of Building Restrictions on Housing Affordability," Federal Reserve Bank of New York, Economic Policy Review, June 2003.

8 C. M. E. Whitehead, "Planning Policies and Affordable Housing," *Housing Studies* 22, no. 1 (2007): 25–44; A. W. Evans, *Economics and Land-Use Planning* (Oxford: Blackwell, 2004).

9 Urban Land Institute–Seattle, "Total Affordability: Meeting the Housing Challenge-Case Studies" August 20, 2009; Margaret Walls and Virginia McConnell, Transfer of Development Rights in U.S. Communities, Resources for the Future, Washington, DC, September 2007.

10 Committee on the Global Financial System, "Housing Finance in the Global Financial Market," Bank for International Settlements, Working Paper No. 26, January 2006.

11 Congressional Budget Office, "An Overview of Federal Support for Housing," November 3, 2009.

12 John McIlwain, "Housing in America: The Next Decade," The Urban Land Institute Trustees Meeting, January 26, 2010; James Barth, et al, *The Mortgage Meltdown and Global Credit Crisis* (New York: John Wiley & Sons, 2009).

13 "Rebooting the Private MBS Market," Mortgage Banking, October 1, 2010.

14 "IFR–Sequoia Deal Bolsters Case for RMBS Revival," Reuters, March 1, 2011.

15 "A Responsible Market for Housing Finance: A Progressive Plan to Reform the U.S. Secondary Market for Residential Mortgages," Mortgage Finance Study Group, Center for American Progress, Washington, DC, January 2011.

16 Peter J. Wallison, Alex J. Pollock, and Edward J. Pinton, "Taking the Government Out of Housing Finance: Principles for Reforming the Housing Finance Market," American Enterprise Institute, Washington, DC, March 24, 2011.

17 Franklin Allen and Glenn Yago, *Financing the Future* (New York: Pearson, 2010).

18 This discussion is largely based on a financial innovations lab conducted for the Ford Foundation in 2009.

19 For other interesting financing models, see Alan Boyce, Glenn Hubbard, and Chris Mayer, "Streamlined Refinancings for up to 30 Million Borrowers," Draft 11, September 1, 2011; and Robert J. Shiller, Rafal M. Wojakowski, M. Shahid Ebrahim, and Mark B. Shackleton, "Continuous Workout Mortgages," Yale University, Cowles Foundation for Research in Economics, Discussion Paper No.1,794, April 2011.

20 Douglas Rice and Barbara Sard, "Decade of Neglect Has Weakened Federal Low-Income Housing Programs," Center for Budget and Policy Priorities, Washington, DC, February 24, 2009.

21 Michael Davies, et al. "Housing Finance Agencies in Asia," *Housing Finance International* (March 2009): 38–40.

22 UN-Habitat, "Community-Based Housing Credit Arrangements in Low Income Housing: Assessment of Potentials and Impacts," Nairobi: UN-Habitat, 2004.

23 G. Landaeta, "Strategies for Low-income Housing, Lund University," Sweden, 2004.

24 Hernando de Soto, *The Mystery of Capital* (New York: Basic Books, 2000).

25 "Housing for All: The Challenges of Affordability, Accessibility and Sustainability: A Synthesis Report," UN Human Settlements Programme, Nairobi, 2008.

26 Davies, et al. (2009).

27 Zaigham Mahmood Rizvi, "Pro-Poor Housing," *Housing Finance International* (Spring 2010): 15–18.

28 S. M. Li and Z. Yi, "Financing Home Purchase in China," *Housing Studies* 22, no. 3 (2007): 409–425

29 L. Chiquier and M. Lea (ed.), *Housing Finance Policy in Emerging Markets* (Washington, DC: World Bank, 2009): 265–277.

30 Janet Xin Ge, "An Alternative Financing Method for Affordable Housing," Housing Finance International, December 2009.

31 "Financial Innovations for Housing: After the Meltdown," Milken Institute, November 2009.

32 "Housing for All" (2008).

33 A. Escobar and S. R. Merrill, "Housing Microfinance: The State of Practice," in eds. F. Daphnis and B. Ferguson, *Housing Microfinance* (Bloomfield, CT: Kumarian Press, 2004).

34 J. Gyntelberg and E. Remolona, "Securitization in Asia and the Pacific: Implications for Liquidity and Credit Risks," Bank of International Settlements Review, June 2006.

35 National Development Council, *Revolving Loan Fund Handbook,* State of California, Department of Housing and Community Development, 2008.

36 A full discussion of all these measures can be found in F. J. Fabozzi and M. Choudhry (eds.), *The Handbook of European Structure Financial Products* (Hoboken, N.J.: John Wiley & Sons, 2004).

37 "Beltway Burden: The Combined Cost of Housing and Transportation in the Washington, D.C. Metropolitan Area," Urban Land Institute Terwilliger Center for Workforce Housing, 2009; "Priced Out: Persistence of Workforce Housing Gaps in the Boston Metropolitan Area," Urban Land Institute Terwilliger Center for Workforce Housing, 2010.

38 McIlwain (2010).

39 John V. Thomas, "Residential Construction Trends in America's Metropolitan Regions," U.S. Environmental Protection Agency, 2009.

40 R. Brown, S. Borgeson, J. Koomey, and P. Biermayer: "U.S. Building-Sector Energy Efficiency Potential," Environmental Energy Technologies Division, Ernest Orlando Lawrence Berkeley National Laboratory, University of California Berkeley, September 2008.

41 "Business Case for Commercializing Sustainable Investment," Capital Markets Briefing Paper, Capital Markets Partnership, Washington, DC, 2009.

42 Much of this discussion is summarized from our "Financing the Residential Retrofit Revolution," Milken Institute Financial Innovations Lab Report (April 2010).

43 "Recovery Through Retrofit," White House Report/Middle Class Task Force, Council on Environmental Quality, October 2009. See www.whitehouse.gov/assets/documents/Recovery_Through_Retrofit_Final_Report.pdf (accessed March 16, 2010).

44 "Financial Assistance Funding Opportunity Announcement," U.S. Department of Energy, October 2009. See www.eecbg.energy.gov/Downloads/EECBGCompetitiveFOA148MON.pdf (accessed March 16, 2010). The Retrofit Ramp-Up application deadline was December 2009; award recipients were notified in March 2010, with awards distributed in May 2010.

45 Property Assessed Clean Energy Policy Brief, 2010.

6

Lessons Learned—
Back to the Future

Financial innovation is imperative for promoting well-functioning housing markets. Changes in the increasing structural demand for capital in housing are demographically driven and shape market structure and performance.

As documented throughout this book, urbanization and household formation have driven financial innovation in housing markets throughout history—from the very first mortgages to covered bonds, guarantees, insurance, tax credits and subsidies, and secondary market development.

Regardless of geography, using cash alone to buy or build housing has long proven overly restrictive and prohibitively expensive. In earlier historical periods, specialized lenders charged interest rates that limited capital access and hindered entry of new participants, such as developers, consumers, and financial intermediaries. Financial innovations then enabled private investors to enter the market, fund development, and create long-term, low-cost sources of capital. All these innovations required reporting, regulation, and oversight.

Securitization contributed to the housing bubble as originators ignored credit risk and underwriting standards disintegrated. However, both directly and through covered bonds and other structured products, securitization lowered funding costs, created sources of capital for borrowers, and expanded opportunities for institutional investors around the world.

Innovative loan products can reduce costs to creditworthy borrowers (either homeowners or rental housing developers), while other products will enable financial institutions to manage risk and free up capital that can be used to meet housing needs.[1]

From the Homestead Act and other nineteenth-century land reforms, to the emergence of secondary mortgage markets and securitization, innovation has been a vital element of housing finance. Market-based finance emerged over the past century and became important throughout the world. It has varied widely in form, mix of instruments, government support, market structure, and types of housing. There is no "one size fits all" version.

Highly regulated and noncompetitive financial systems have been curtailed as the importance of property rights became more widely recognized through land reform, land registries, and collateralization. With greater access to capital, the cost of financing has fallen, making homeownership and rental housing more affordable over the past century. The increased availability and range of mortgage products for homebuyers and developers, combined with structured finance, created greater liquidity in real estate markets and drove trillions of dollars of investment into this sector. Moreover, mortgage-equity withdrawals have contributed greatly to credit availability and, hence, aggregate consumption.[2]

During the recent housing bubble, however, home prices went far above what average families could afford. Public and business policies that eased lending requirements and led to more lax and less transparent underwriting standards seriously slanted debt-to-equity ratios. As more mortgage defaults and foreclosures ensued, liquidity constraints in markets collapsed the housing price bubble. As credit markets froze and contagion spread throughout the financial sector, the macroeconomic conditions that had encouraged growth and shelter-access disappeared.

Housing markets, structured finance, and mortgage-backed securities functioned properly when transparent information, independent analysis, and standardized reporting were available. But as conformity and opaque reporting replaced transparency—and as mortgage originators became detached from the consequences of erratic lending due to perverse incentives—undesirable outcomes spread. Housing markets and prices collapsed. The wisdom of crowds was replaced by the madness of mobs in the mortgage marketplace. As investors fled, market deterioration compounded further.

As government oversight weakened, excessive leverage (Securities and Exchange Commission [SEC] deregulation of investment banks in 2005 allowed leverage to more than double) and overly complex financial products enabled some banks to evade capital requirements. New mortgage-collateralized debt obligations created problems for rating agencies, and investors swept the market.[3]

New waves of housing demand have broken into the markets, and recent crises raise new questions: What is the appropriate role for government in the housing market? How can housing markets operate more efficiently? What can be learned from mistakes of the past?

In all the banking and financial crises we have studied, periods of initial financial liberalization and prosperity in real estate markets drove demand to peaks that led to regulatory failures, overpricing, and shoddy risk analysis.[4] Our review of the long sweep of housing finance history yields the following lessons, which are consistent across time in developed and emerging markets alike.

Lesson 1: Don't Compromise on Credit Analysis

As demand for mortgage-backed securities outstripped supply and inflated home values, guidelines designed to ease credit failed. Fundamental analysis was neglected, increasing information asymmetries among all parties in the housing market (largely through principal-agent conflicts that drive moral hazard and adverse selection).

Nearly $20 trillion in mortgages originated during the period of easy credit from 2003 to 2008. Before 2007, when housing prices began to decline, residential real estate was estimated at $60 trillion; by 2011, it had declined to $50 trillion. Much wealth was destroyed in Spain, Ireland, and numerous other European countries, as well as the United States.

Whether attempting to fund new housing in emerging countries or trying to understand the complexities of collateralized debt obligations (CDOs), clear and unambiguous information is essential.

Investors need to know about titles, financial accounts, deeds, and contracts. This information makes it possible to determine value, assess risks, and track performance. As Hernando de Soto states, "[W]ithout standardization, the values of assets and relationships are so variable that they can't be used to guarantee credit, to generate mortgages and bundle them into securities, to represent them in shares to raise capital."[5]

Clear property rights are vital to expand access to affordable housing—whether owned or rented—in emerging or developed markets. Property rights facilitate housing credit by establishing clear collateral and legal claims. Transparent real estate laws are also critical for effective credit analysis and allocation.

Weakly underwritten instruments and private securitizations (which government agencies later absorbed during the crisis) increased borrowers' incentives to default, due to their limited equity and lenders' lack of adequate recourse. The proliferation of new and flexible mortgage products alone was not the primary cause of the market failure. Instead, the abbreviated loan process and abandonment of long-proven underwriting standards destined many of those products to fail.

Underwriting ignored transaction costs (escrow taxes, insurance, and so on) enabled loan-to-value ratios above historically proven safe limits and resulted in automated and unverified valuation models. The resulting layering of risk—based on deceptive credit terms, financial illiteracy, or fraud by borrowers—led to a flood of credit on unreasonable terms.

These failings led to the explosion of moral hazard, which ultimately pushed the costs of excessive risk onto taxpayers. Foreclosures, delinquencies, and negative equity left an unprecedented number of vacant homes, increasing downward pressure on values in struggling neighborhoods.

Lesson 2: Flexible Capital Structure Matters

Financially sustainable capital structures for the housing market require a balance of debt *and* equity. Early innovations in savings for housing, such as the building societies discussed in Chapter 2, "Building Blocks of Modern Housing Finance," developed a method for collectively accumulating equity to support long-term lending. These pioneering principles were later embedded in government entities, nonprofit organizations, formal financial institutions, and home-savings products. Lessons from those earliest models of peer-to-peer lending can be applied to today's crisis in developed economies and growing demand in emerging and frontier markets. New investment vehicles can arise from old innovations.[6]

Since the Great Depression, long-term (20–30 years), fixed-rate mortgages have financed homeownership and enabled developers to provide affordable rental housing. This innovation sprang from the failure of earlier capital structures in housing and the absence of long-term, low-cost loans.

After the saturation of the housing market in the U.S. in 1925, lending standards were loosened as property values rose. Homes were bought with short-term loans (three to five years) requiring 50% equity payments. Many buyers took out secondary loans to pay for the primary loan and purchase price. The classic mistake of financing long-term housing assets with short-term credit, coupled with inadequate equity, led to massive defaults and delinquencies as values declined.

When the market collapsed in the Great Depression, the federal government intervened by offering refinancing through the creation of the Home Owners Loan Corporation. Later the Federal Housing Administration provided broader mortgage insurance, which enabled the absorption of excess inventory and restored the flow of credit. Extended loan maturities became the new standard in real estate markets in the U.S. and abroad.

With proper underwriting, the 30-year, fixed-rate mortgage increased the supply of sustainable credit. The alignment of interests among homebuyers, developers, and lenders continued under conditions that enabled liquidity, standardization, and transparency.

As we've shown, rebooting securitization with retained-interest transactions by originators, introducing covered bonds, and dealing with other gaps in the market's capital structure are vital to reinventing housing finance. Loan-modification programs, debt-for-equity swaps that allow rent-to-own as an alternative to foreclosure, and encouragement of investor finance could also be helpful.[7] All these measures could improve liquidity over the longer term.

New policies and programs that enable shared equity, flexibility in mortgage refinancing, and lower transaction costs in finance for homeownership and rental housing can overcome the frictions that have hampered monetary policy, inflated foreclosures, and slowed economic recovery.[8]

Lesson 3: Size Matters

Supersized mortgages and houses led to much of the overleveraging and sprawling developments that made housing unaffordable. According to the Census Bureau, the average new home sold in the U.S. ballooned in size over the last three decades, from 1,700 square feet to 2,422. That's a 42% increase, with the trend intensifying since the late 1990s.

"McMansions" had nothing to do with making room for more kids. (The average size of the American household fell from 2.76 people in 1980 to 2.57 in 2009.) Instead, rising home prices lured some consumers into an over-reliance on housing as an investment; they built homes that were larger than needed and harder to maintain, with the anticipation that they could serve as a giant savings account, with the added benefit of appreciation.[9] Taste may also have been a factor in the shift to larger homes.

What if houses returned to the size expected by the typical U.S. homebuyer 30 years ago? The average new home would have been 722 square feet smaller in 2009. If you consider the average cost per square foot, returning to the expectations of our parents' generation would have produced a savings of $80,000 per home in 2009 alone. America's total expenditures on all new homes sold over the past 30 years would have been $1.2 trillion less in today's dollars, and that savings would continue to accrue in the future. That's before taking into account the cost of furnishing, heating, cooling, and cleaning all that extra space.

Today Americans devote 34% of their household expenditures to their homes. But if Americans are willing to rethink their assumptions about what their houses should be, they could radically improve the lives of those who live in those homes.

The relationships among housing size, suburbanization, and exurbanization, and the demand of increased energy inputs have created costs that should be factored into twenty-first-century credit analysis.

Factors such as neighborhood compactness, access to public transit, and rates of vehicle ownership affect mortgage performance. There is a direct, statistically significant link between longer, costlier commuting and a higher risk of default.[10] Transportation and energy costs take a growing toll on disposable income as urban settlement patterns are increasingly dispersed. Roughly 17% of an average U.S. household income goes to transportation costs, so mortgage underwriting procedures should consider this factor as it relates to financial risk.

Mixed use and diversification that accompany location efficiency are also key factors in stabilizing housing markets. Diversification by income levels, use (retail and residential), and tenure (rental and ownership) attract different elements of demand that result in more sustainable communities. Reduced isolation, labor market access, and other elements that strengthen social capital in communities appear to bolster financial and environmental sustainability as well.[11]

Lesson 4: Structured Products and Secondary Markets Work

If lenders and investors monitor credit quality and if timely, adequate information is provided, securitization works well. Beyond the product, market, and regulatory failures previously noted, the ability to securitize (with proper risk retention by originators to align interests) is central to housing finance. The link between risk management and capital access for housing has been historically demonstrated.

Secondary markets expand liquidity and help to balance the broader costs and risks of housing finance. They provide access to capital across market segments (including low- and moderate-income borrowers), types (owner-occupied and rental housing), geographies (urban and rural), and originators (including credit unions, micro lenders in developing countries, and community-based lenders). Providing a wide range of product choices to borrowers can achieve the link between housing finance and macroeconomic growth policy.

As information technology, data reporting, and regulatory transparency become more widespread, the transitions to recovering secondary markets and securitization will succeed without sacrificing stability.

For housing to be affordable and sustainable, securitization, covered bonds, and other hybrid products are required. Long-term, fixed-rate mortgages require liquidity in real estate financing. Capital markets have proven fundamental to this process, insofar as they enable the diversification of risk for investors while avoiding its reconcentration on financial institution balance sheets, as occurred in the most recent crisis.

When successful, regulatory measures ensure benefits to renters, owners, and developers in single-family and multifamily housing. Government guarantees and subsidies could enable sustainable financial innovation by private, nonprofit, and public investors. New products and delivery modes for housing construction, access, and retrofitting are discussed in Chapter 4, "Housing Finance in the Emerging Economies," and Chapter 5, "Future Innovations in Housing Finance."

Final Remarks

Beyond the economic characteristics of housing as a physical structure providing shelter and investment value to consumers lays the broader meaning of homes and the hopes and dreams tied to them. Our hope in this book is to provide a guide to the workings of the troubled global housing markets and an inventory of the financial toolkit necessary to fix them. As the housing crisis in the developing world and the major disruptions in developed markets prove, no quick fixes or applications can be cut and pasted into vastly different demographics, economic environments, and capital markets. Nonetheless, the principles of housing finance remain consistent, achievable, and available to guide the creation of affordable homes and sustainable communities to better serve society's interests.

Endnotes

1 Edmund S. Phelps and Leo M. Tilman, "Wanted: A First National Bank of Innovation," *Harvard Business Review* (January/February 2010): 102–103.

2 John V. Ducka, et. al., "How Financial Innovations and Accelerators Drive Booms and Busts in U.S. Consumption," Federal Reserve Bank of Dallas Working Paper, May 2011.

3 For more detail see, Franklin Allen and Glenn Yago, *Financing the Future*, New York: Pearson, 2010; James R. Barth, Tong Li, Wenling Lu, Triphon Phumiwasana, and Glenn Yago, *The Rise and Fall of the U.S. Mortgage and Credit Markets: A Comprehensive Analysis of the Meltdown* (New York: John Wiley & Sons, 2009).

4 James R. Barth, Daniel E. Nolle, Triphon Phumiwasana, and Glenn Yago, "A Cross-Country Analysis of the Bank Supervisory Framework and Bank Performance," *Financial Markets, Institutions & Instruments* 12, no. 2 (2003):.67–120.

5 Hernando de Soto, "The Destruction of Economic Facts," *Bloomberg Businessweek,* April 28, 2011.

6 Peter Tufano and Daniel Schneider, "Using Financial Innovation to Support Savers: From Coercion to Excitement," in *Insufficient Funds: Savings, Assets, Credit and Banking Among Low-Income Households,* ed. Rebecca Blank and Michael Barr (New York: Russell Sage, 2008); Peter Tufano and Daniel Schneider, "New Savings from Old Innovations: Asset Building for the Less Affluent," in *Financing Low-Income Communities,* ed. Julia S. Rubin (New York: Russell Sage, 2007).

7 Lewis S. Ranieri, Kenneth T. Rosen, Andrea Lepcio, and Buck Collins, "Plan B: A Comprehensive Approach to Moving Housing, Households and the Economy Forward," Ranieri Partners Management and Rosen Consulting, April 4, 2011.

8 David Milkes and Vladimir Pillonca, "Financial Innovation and European Housing and Mortgage Markets," *Oxford Review of Economic Policy* 24, no. 1 (2008): 176–179.

9 James Barth, Tong Li, and Rick Palacios, "McMansion Economics," *Los Angeles Times*, November 21, 2010.

10 Stephanie Yatos Rauterkus, Grant Thall, and Eric Hangen, "Location Efficiency and Mortgage Default," *Journal of Sustainable Real Estate*, in press.

11 Loretta Lees, "Gentrification and Social Mixing: Towards an Inclusive Urban Renaissance," Urban Studies 45, no. 12 (2008): 2,449–2,476.

INDEX

C

post-crisis housing markets,
140-141
PPP (purchasing power
parity), 115
Preemption Act of 1841, 16
preserving affordability, 152
pricing
in China, 116-119
innovative pricing models,
149-150
prime mortgage foreclosures, 87
prime mortgage originations,
80, 87
PRIs (program-related
investments), 151
private investors, restoring
partnership with, 145-146
private mortgage insurance
(PMI), 43-44
program-related investments
(PRIs), 151
property logjam, clearing, 150
property rights, importance
of, 174
property tax-based financing,
164-170
purchasing power parity
(PPP), 115

R

Recovery Through Retrofit
plan, 165
regulation of conventional
mortgage lenders, 58-60
residential delinquency rates,
U.S. versus Canada, 97
restoration of partnership with
private investors, 145-146
rethinking size of housing,
176-177

Revenue Act of 1951, 35
Revenue Act of 1962, 35
reverse mortgages, 5
revolving loan funds, 156-157
Riegle-Neal Interstate Banking
and Branching Efficiency
Act, 63
Russia
mortgage market
characteristics, 113
source of funding for home
mortgages, 110

S

savings and loan associations
founding of, 9
FSLIC (Federal Savings
and Loan Insurance
Corporation), 33
history of
*first hundred years
(1830-1930), 25-31
founding of, 8
Great Depression, 31-33
postwar growth and
diversification, 33-36
turbulence of 1980s, 36-37*
national institutions, 28
nonfarm residential mortgage
holdings, by type of institution
(1900-2010), 30
shifting of interest-rate risk to
borrowers, 70-71
U.S. League of Local Building
and Loan Associations, 28
savings models, 154-155
secondary markets, value of,
177-178
Section 203(b) mortgages, 41-45,
56-59

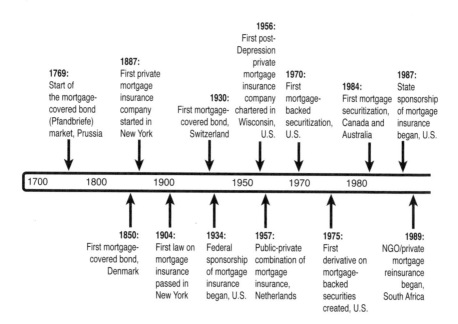

1769:
Start of the mortgage-covered bond (Pfandbriefe) market, Prussia

1887:
First private mortgage insurance company started in New York

1930:
First mortgage-covered bond, Switzerland

1956:
First post-Depression private mortgage insurance company chartered in Wisconsin, U.S.

1970:
First mortgage-backed securitization, U.S.

1984:
First mortgage securitization, Canada and Australia

1987:
State sponsorship of mortgage insurance began, U.S.

1700   1800   1900   1950   1970   1980

1850:
First mortgage-covered bond, Denmark

1904:
First law on mortgage insurance passed in New York

1934:
Federal sponsorship of mortgage insurance began, U.S.

1957:
Public-private combination of mortgage insurance, Netherlands

1975:
First derivative on mortgage-backed securities created, U.S.

1989:
NGO/private mortgage reinsurance began, South Africa